Grace is greater than

Samantha Nelson

WESTBOW
PRESS®
A DIVISION OF THOMAS NELSON
& ZONDERVAN

Scripture taken from the Holy Bible, NEW INTERNATIONAL VERSION®.
Copyright © 1973, 1978, 1984 by Biblica, Inc. All rights reserved worldwide.
Used by permission. NEW INTERNATIONAL VERSION® and NIV® are
registered trademarks of Biblica, Inc. Use of either trademark for the offering
of goods or services requires the prior written consent of Biblica US, Inc.

WestBow Press books may be ordered through booksellers or by contacting:

WestBow Press
A Division of Thomas Nelson & Zondervan
1663 Liberty Drive
Bloomington, IN 47403
www.westbowpress.com
1 (866) 928-1240

Because of the dynamic nature of the Internet, any web addresses or
links contained in this book may have changed since publication and
may no longer be valid. The views expressed in this work are solely those
of the author and do not necessarily reflect the views of the publisher,
and the publisher hereby disclaims any responsibility for them.

Any people depicted in stock imagery provided by Thinkstock are
models, and such images are being used for illustrative purposes only.
Certain stock imagery © Thinkstock.

ISBN: 978-1-5127-2163-8 (sc)
ISBN: 978-1-5127-2165-2 (hc)
ISBN: 978-1-5127-2164-5 (e)

Library of Congress Control Number: 2015919469

Print information available on the last page.

WestBow Press rev. date: 11/19/2015

Contents

Dedication

To those people who even without realising it encouraged me to keep on dreaming big, to keep fighting for what I want and to keep praising God, even in the hallways.

Preface

The words on these pages have been inspired by the words of life on different pages, in a different book. They were typed during events in my life that left me with no room to do anything else but to share what happened. They were intrinsically put together in a lifetime's events by the creator in an existence that he wants to share with *you* because you are without a doubt worth every hour, every sleepless night, every drama and hurt.

My life and this book is dedicated to letting you know that you are loved, no matter where you are, no matter what you are doing or what you have done, no matter who you are, or who you think you are and most importantly whether you feel it or not.

Demichael, no matter what we have been through, no matter what we go through, it will be used for a greater purpose, and even if I had choice of the whole world, who has been and who is to come. I would still pick you. Cheeseball.

MaMa, I would not be half the person I am without your courage to follow what is right, what is true and what is love, so thankful that you never fail to inspire me.

Poppa Joe, without your investment where would I be? Thank you for always coming to my rescue, no matter where in the world I was.

My favourite little man, you are not so little anymore, and without you I wouldn't know what I was capable of. Thank you for bringing out the best in me. Thank you for bringing Dom into my life, what a sister and friend I have in her!

Acknowledgement

Jesus, you already have one book dedicated to your life, but this is a book dedicated to you living in me. You worked through so many different people to reach me and love me, and how could I not acknowledge that?

Everyone needs a James Eller in their life. He has spent countless hours working with me to encourage and edit the passion that pours out on paper. I remember at one point people were confused as to what was going on, but it was just your dedication to my vision! Thankful for friends like you!

Introduction

"There is nothing more beautiful than the way the ocean refuses to stop kissing the shoreline no matter how many times it is sent away." Doesn't this remind you a lot of God's love? I am sure if you ask various people who have come into my life, they will tell you they feel a lot like the Ocean too, or have in the past. I think we all have people placed specifically in our lives and no matter what we do or say to them they still love us and care for us a lot like God. It's so humbling to be reminded that it doesn't matter what happens, God's love is bigger than anything, literally anything we will ever face! And it is the same yesterday, today, and forever! Mind blowing!

Before deciding to write this, I had so much stuff going on-I am a bit of a nerd like that. I even got into a habit of reading my Bible (well a lot more than I had ever done before). In my opinion, I basically lived like an ancient Scholar, to the point where I even compared myself to Paul writing his letters to the early church … in my dreams! But Paul suffered and I feel like I have been down a path of suffering. I was facing what I thought to be the biggest trial I could and would face and nothing but the word satisfied my cravings. Little did I know that this was just the beginning of things. I felt like I was in a helpless place and disliked the fact that I could not be around people I loved like I was use to; to share the understanding of the amazing Love of God . There is something comforting about being around Christians. However, sometimes what we don't realise in those seasons is there are multiple ways to share the Light of the word and pass the love of God on to people that haven't seen or felt it, or even feel unworthy of it. A great deal of the time, we completely disregard the people we don't know like litter in the street. I think that it can be really convenient for us to share something we are passionate about with those we relate to on a personal level, but kindness is suggested to be something the deaf can hear and the blind can see. This means that we should not stop only with those who are involved in our daily lives but even with those who are unreachable. I often have conversations with my friends, making up excuses of why NOT to do something. This is usually why I shouldn't write and share the conversations between my spirit and the spirit of God -the so beautiful and personal conversations that they have when I am in the manifest presence of my favourite. I constantly felt like I didn't have enough life experience to tell other people about my walk with God. However, as I continued to work on this book and experience the things I have, it is coming more and more to light that God will constantly prove us wrong. It is in our weaknesses and our experience (or 'lack of experience') that he will creep into the crevices of life and shine that ever bright light.

One particular response to this was almost typical for my friend Kemar. He told me I was a crazy woman and that I should write about moving to America and meeting the man of my dreams. At that point I felt urged to remind him that I didn't just meet the man of my dreams, I fell in love. Not only with Demichael, but with Jesus too. And it struck me … I, along with every other Christian to walk this planet in the past and in the years to come, am a Living Testimony of God's love. And boy was this love a testimony!

Love is suggested to be an intense feeling of deep affection or a deep attachment to someone else. This statement alone is enough to make someone feel vulnerable. And the 'me' of merely twenty years old did everything within her power to feel anything but vulnerable.

The words Love, Relationship, Marriage, Children, and Family were not very likely to come out of my mouth. If they did, they were more than likely to cause goose pimples, and possibly even spine shivers, than an overflow of joy, or peace, within my heart. It was a swinging brick. Nevertheless, this is my story of how God performed an amazing miracle and brought me back to life using the strangest of situations.

CHAPTER 1

True Love

It doesn't matter where I start or finish with any kind of study of Scripture or literature, but the lesson that I have learned the most is that everything should always be brought back to love. It is more than apparent in each and every single one of these teachings that everything rests on the word *love* and on our ability to love. This was a severely difficult thing for someone who did not believe in the power of love and who, therefore, did not believe in the power of God. The Bible tells us that God is love, so did that mean I didn't believe in God? Disbelief in the power of God often leads us, as humans, to say, "Show me, and I will trust." On the other hand, God tells us to trust, and he will be more than happy to show us. What I have also realised is that this inability to fully depend on something we cannot see comes from the suit of flesh we sport, just as my inability to believe in the love of God is not something new—not only in my own life, but in the history of life. Jesus's disciples (those who followed his every move) listened to his every word and did not believe in the promises he had made them until they came face to face with the answers. Then there was no more room for denial.

"Now Thomas (called Didymus), one of the Twelve, was not with the disciples when Jesus came. So the other disciples told him,

"We have seen the Lord!"

But he said to them, "Unless I see the nail marks in his hands and put my finger where the nails were, and put my hand into his side, I will not believe it."

A week later His disciples were in the house again, and Thomas was with them. Though the doors were locked, Jesus came and stood among them and said,

"Peace be with you!" Then he said to Thomas "Put your finger here; see my hands. Reach out your hand and put it into my side. Stop doubting and believe."

Thomas said to him, "My Lord and my God!"

Then Jesus told him, "Because you have seen me, you have believed; blessed are those who have not seen and yet have believed." (John 20:24–29)

The book of John depicts Jesus's love for us, and this particular Scripture is one of my favourites. It is easy to imagine Jesus as this almost angel type person who came and did not have to face the things that we face—He didn't have to cry. He rarely laughed. When he was a child, he didn't fall and scrape his knees. We hear the stories, yet we find it so difficult to comprehend his humility. However, Jesus shows his understanding of the flesh and how it is difficult to believe in something that we do not see. It speaks to us on a personal level that Jesus came as a human being, giving up his throne in heaven, to live life like we have to live life, to face each and every last temptation that we face under the schemes of Satan, and to show us his understanding of the fall and how he, the King of Kings, loved us so much that he walked alongside us as the Son of Man. What a beautiful picture of love! How can that not be enough for someone to fall deeply in love with Jesus?

Often, the difference between *what is* and *what could be* isn't about how far we have to go to reach it or what we have to do to understand it. It is about the resistance we have in our head that tells us it cannot be possible or that it cannot be true. It is very apparent that Jesus understands how the earth we co-inhabit can have an effect on the gray matter within our skull. He does not have to prove himself to anyone, but by grace itself says, "Look Thomas. Now follow!" This is something that had to happen to me, not just once, or even twice, but multiple times for me to see God's outstretched arms welcoming me into the family.

I did not grow up in a Christian family, but I was blessed with a loving, caring, compassionate family. One that nurtured me, protected me, cared for me, and loved me to the best of their ability. Nonetheless, for me this was never enough; and although that sounds ungrateful now, it was never intended to be that way. It was when I found myself in desperate situations, where God worked undoubtable miracles, that I felt there was no more room for denying a God who is passionate about me. A God who sent his spirit so many times to knock on my door. A God who was standing there those eighteen years waiting for me to reach out for his hand. The phrase "ignorance can kill" has never been so true to me. However, through God's grace, a woman who I regard as my spiritual mother—or as my Godmother—continued to press in. She had God's strength and resources to enable her to reach the lost, and she chose to love me even when I didn't deserve her love—just like we don't deserve God's love. His amazing grace and mercy already have this covered.

As humans, we are very inclined to overlook, or even bury, negative mindsets as something we will "get over" or "grow out of," but like everything else, these negative mindsets have an origin that usually has a negative stigma attached to the root. Until this is destroyed, the Enemy has a foothold that is not a part of the promise we have. We have already won the war, and the almighty God declared it to be good! It is due to these negative mindsets that we begin to build up the walls barricading our hearts within our chests away from the destruction of the world and away from the grip of the evil and the peril of hurt. What we fail to realise is that God doesn't want anything from us; he simply wants us. We are confined by the walls we ourselves build. If we spent more time focusing on the one who is bigger than all of it, opposed to the problem itself, we would live in faith instead of fear. However, until you have seen God's love, this is something you are probably clueless about. And this I was until the age of ten.

Growing up wasn't necessarily tough for me, or so I thought. My parents were family orientated and they strived to provide the best for my brother and me. We spent countless weekends with my cousins and grandparents. For the majority of this time, both of my parents were out of work. They did everything within their power to ensure smooth sailing through my first five years of life. At the age of five, my brother was born. At the time, I thought it was amazing. And to this day, I still do think he is a pretty amazing guy. Without a doubt, he is one of the biggest blessings in my life—as much as I don't admit it. It was at this time, however, where my family situation began to deteriorate. My father found full-time employment in a factory that was enough to suck the life out of anyone, and my mother did the best she could in her situation raising two young children. It was during this time that she started suffering from severe migraines. She would be bed bound for days—thus leaving six-year-old, blonde-haired, blue-eyed me to hold down the fort. I don't particularly remember doing so until around the age of nine, which is where my abhorrence for my mother's illness and my father's job originated. When my parents were able, they did the best they could at raising my brother and me. This account by no means belittles the effort and love they put into both of our lives. However, there and then, at the age of nine, I had a lot of growing up to do. I became the little mother of the household. I remember cooking and cleaning to the best of my little ability. And I remember bossing my brother around, which, at the time, I do remember thoroughly enjoying. But looking back now, all I really wanted was to be childlike with no responsibilities.

Hardship often prepares ordinary people for extraordinary destinies; you have heard it before, and God is the God of the extraordinary. I am not suggesting here that I have had a hard life. I have learned how to hold my own and strive for the things I want in life, because no one was about to get up and chase my dreams for me. This gave me ambition to chase after things, to never give up, to take everything into my own ability, and to do what I could to change or fix a situation. I never appreciated what I had. I always wanted more. Over these past few months and years, Jesus has made it more and more apparent to me now that happiness does not come to those who don't appreciate what they already have. Happiness, for me, came in recognition, which usually resulted in a financial outpour from whatever direction I could find—or even just a comment about how I had done an amazing job. One thing that did bring me happiness was when people came to me to help them with things. This was the best kind of recognition of *my* own ability—that they thought I was good enough to help them with a situation. I never found myself secure in what I had. I always wanted more. And as human beings, more often than not, we do want more. We see our cup as half empty opposed to half full.

Today, many of the enemies we face are not flesh and blood, and not even of the evil spirits of this dark world, but are within ourselves. Internally, we face a battle greater than anything. The best thing the Enemy can do is to turn it back to self. During this time, as a ten year old, I developed the ability to 'self-pity', a term I use loosely now because I regard it as a tactical way I used to receive attention. At that time, it was attention that I craved!

Grace > Feelings

CHAPTER 2

Saving grace

The depiction of 'saving grace' came into my life when I was ten years old. I often watched my brother whilst my Mum visited my grandparents. As children, we would rather be out playing than sitting in their house and struggling to please everyone. My Mum would give in to us, but ensure that I watched my five year old brother. My family house is located at the top of a very large hill. Half way down this hill is a park which as a child was the best thing *ever*! It had everything you could ever imagine or want from a park right on your doorstep. I swear when I was little I thought it was heaven! Children often have a fearless nature. Nothing fazes them. Nothing! And I have witnessed this myself, as an adult now, but also on that day as a ten year old. I remember, growing up, my brother was a fearless rogue and would do crazy things, like literally the most ridiculous things. We were always in the hospital because he had either decided to set himself on fire or had dared one of his friends to ride over his legs on a bike, or whatever ridiculous thing you can imagine. This one day, he sat on his skateboard at the top of the hill. I wasn't particularly worried. In fact, I think he was only receiving maybe five percent of my attention at the time, if that. But I do remember the next few moments vividly though. You couldn't have predicted it if you tried. It was like something from a movie! They say God's timing is perfect; well this was beyond perfect. The exact moment my brother reaches the bottom of the hill, so does a car. Not only the car, but my mother as well. As my brother slips smoothly under the car, the driver slams the brakes. My mother screams, I shut my eyes, and a complete stranger set off sprinting down the street. It was actually unbelievable how the events slipped right into place. Only typical to my life, my brother pulls out from under the car perfectly fine, looking incredibly innocent and angelic. The driver suffered more stress and anxiety issues than Matthew physical injuries. My mother grabs his arm and checks him up and down to make sure he's okay. The stranger arrives panicked, asking if everything is okay. Before my mum can say anything, she looks at me. Those eyes pierced my soul! I knew what was coming next and I was dreading it more than you could even imagine! My life flashed before my eyes, which at ten years old, it did, but it didn't last long. I don't even remember what my mother said to me. It was as if someone had blasted me with a big gush of air, one of those powerful ones that you use to blow leaves off the pavement. I was blown off my feet! In the bad books. Probably never to leave my bedroom again! Luckily that day, God sent someone who would go on to protect me for years and years to come. Although I did deserve the trouble I should have been in, this person wasn't just to save me from a severe punishment, she was to save me from myself. Louise Smith of 6 Fair View told my mother off. In front of me. It was like the best thing that could have happened! (Sorry mum, this isn't meant to sound awful; just imagine how I felt at ten!) I remember throwing a silent party. Being bemused by the situation, but knowing my mum probably wasn't going to say too much more. Louise told my mum that it wasn't my fault and that she shouldn't punish me. She said that accidents happen and everyone was okay! She then consoled the driver, who had been sitting there for what must have been the longest two minutes of his life, sending him on his poor old way. At this point, I was still throwing a silent party and regaining my life back in my own little mind. She then turned to me and asked if I wanted to go to McDonald's with them as they were celebrating her eldest daughter Hannah's birthday. It was as if nothing ever happened; it was insane! This was an offer I couldn't refuse! From there on out, I have had someone in my life that you cannot replace. Someone that has become a very close friend. No one will ever replace my mum or my family, but she understood me. I could see it in her eyes. I could feel it standing three meters away. She knew how I was feeling and she didn't have to ask. That day, I gained a mentor, four extra sisters, and an extra brother. And for this, I am eternally grateful. I like to think that they all gained an older sibling, but you will have to ask them about that. They did, however, gain a little ten year old for the rest of the summer holidays, because I don't think a day passed that summer where I didn't end up at 6 Fair View. That is still one of my favourite summers to this day.

My God Mum's house has always been a little bit like a foster home or a halfway house. She has had people in and out of the house for as long as I can remember and I understand why. That's the way God uses her, to show his love through her. She is as patient and understanding as Jesus, and her loyalty to her children is nothing short of biblical. That summer, I regained a childhood. I was allowed to fool around. I made salt dough for the first time. I went on adventures in the forest. We found flowers that we thought had never been found before, so we wrote to the queen. We had endless trips to McDonald's! And we just had plain, sailing, covered in dirt, hilarious fun! This happened to be my last summer, until a lot older, that I chose to be childlike. At the age of eleven, Alcohol slithered its way into my life. I started secondary school (high school), made new friends, and had something to prove. Although I would never change my teenage years, and would never say I didn't have fun, I would never recommend those years to anybody. What was fun and games turned into a dependency that only God could redeem. Although I continued on my regular visits with my God mum, I lived for the weekend. I was no longer innocent or naive to the world. I saved the money my parents would give me for lunch and would ask some strange person going in the off licence to kindly buy me three litres of the cheapest cider to go share with my friends. Although a part of me still enjoyed visiting my God mum and spending time with the kids, the Enemy had caught me with his dazzling offers of popularity, fun and games, and actually, now thinking back, nothing solid. Nothing definite or firm.

Sometimes, it is so easy to be motivated by the stigma attached to being a Christian, to the positive response you get when you're telling people the reason for your actions. It's easy to follow the signs and wonders that God brings. It's easy to say, "*show me,* and I will follow." I am not condemning those who see gold dust and Manna, and other such amazing biblical miracles on earth. I'm saying it becomes a problem when that is our focus and drive for the kingdom. Lucifer focused more on the gifts God is willing to give than God himself. Ezekiel describes Satan to be covered in Sardius, topaz, diamond, beryl, onyx, jasper, sapphire, turquoise, emerald, and gold. How eye catching that must be! How tempting it must have been to follow him, his eye catching promises! What I think Satan really is, is a temperamental fixation, a 'ten minute wonder'. It takes him little to no time to tempt you. However, these temptations are a little like the toys you get at Christmas as a child. Amazing, colourful, loud toys that you would play with for ten minutes until you were bored. This is something my father forever moaned about. As kids, we would ask for things and then in minutes literally get bored. My brother was much more interested with taking things apart or playing in the boxes that the toys that were bought were referred to as ten minute wonders. They break and bring tears, they run out of batteries and are discarded, they become 'old fashioned' so we move onto the next best thing. They are never really as satisfying as we think they will be when we see them in their splendour, shining at us like a pearl on the ocean floor, or the sunlight dancing off the walls. Therefore, people who follow temptations could be compared to magpies, never actually content with what they have, but wanting 'shiny' items to build up their home because they look good. Adding them to the structure and foundation of life will not support you. This comes by lifelong commitment, not just to Jesus, but to the people you are investing in. The people you have agreed to do life with. The people who are silently in the background putting in and putting in. But as a church, you need to draw around those people and support them. We are not called to be a 'ten minute wonder' generation. We are made for more than that. When we say we are going to help, we should help! You need to build your house upon a rock, with a good foundation. Jesus is the love that makes our foundations solid! He infiltrates our every being and satisfies us beyond human belief. And this foundation was set for me when I was ten years old. However, Satan had a different plan.

Grace > being a 'Christian'

CHAPTER 3

Entering the Promised Land

Serving God should not be a chore. It should not be a hobby passed on from generation to generation, a lifestyle to reap benefits, an excuse for pain and sorrow, or something you take part in one day a week. You have to fall in love with God. And once you have done this, you have the key, the key that opens doors of peace and joy and promises from centuries ago that are still true to us today. This key opens the door to heaven on earth; the keys to your heart are the keys to the Kingdom. Once we see it as a love story with our own love letter, things happen. Miracles occur. Miracles as simple as waking to see another day to as big as the price paid on the cross. When people serve the Lord because they love him, it opens a whole new dimension to the possibilities he has given us. To the promises and to the future. And it is by using our love story to instruct us how to put one foot in front of the other that we see all the brilliance from above unfold in front of our very eyes. Like a flower opening in spring petal by petal. Like a duckling hatching and taking his very first steps. This is something it took a long time for me to realise, but when it did, it hit me like a tonne of bricks, right smack bang in the middle of the face. People surround new Christians and expect them to get it right away, to be convicted of everything they were convicted of after all their years of learning. Give them time! I finally realised what it was I was living for, what my purpose here on Earth is: to love and be loved. What I'm not saying is that if you are dedicated to your church, God is disappointed. What I am saying is that if you are not doing this out of love, from the deepest place in your heart, maybe you should question your motive. Why do you serve the Lord? Originally, this lack of love pushed me from the straight path that God had already laid out for me to a path where there wasn't all that much love at all. Meaning the tie I had to God wasn't cement, wasn't strong enough to help me bloom like a rose into his child. When I first started church, everything was new to me. I was like a sponge and I couldn't soak up enough of 'God' and the word and worship and helping out whomever, whenever I could. I suffered hunger pangs for knowing more about the Lord. But this wasn't a revelation. It was an inquisitive nature. My fascination is what kept me at church. I did not truly understand what it meant to follow God. I had not had an encounter that changed my perspective of the term grace because all I knew was that it had saved me that one time. However, the more we meet with grace in our daily lives, the more our greeting to the rest of the world is Jesus. This encounter then encouraged me to turn into a false representation of myself. I quickly slipped into being a puppet and I wasn't necessarily hungry for God but rather hungry for more of a knowledge about this God and the amazing things that he had to offer, the incredible miracles that he was said to perform. I let everyone tell me how I should behave because I lacked that wisdom from the Holy Spirit. I wasn't quite aware of the fact that God is alive and working in and around me right now. Though this was done in love, it wasn't what God had intended. He wants us to be nurtured into the person he created us to be, and that can only be done in love. It can only be done by Him, knowing Him, and understanding he wants a very real, very personal, very unique relationship with us. We have to know and love God *personally*, to watch him change us into the best version of ourselves, and this doesn't happen overnight. As my big brother Jerome would say, "Rome wasn't built in a day." The person I turned into was a very forced, stereotypical version of the follower of Christ I thought I should be, because I hadn't quite encountered God for myself. I hadn't quite met with him on a level or relation or understood that he is alive and he is well. At the time, I did thoroughly enjoy church. I loved the new friends I had made. When I decided to make the commitment, it was evident that the people I spent the most of my time with were not the best influence on my life. Although dear friends, the decision to cut them out of my friendship circle was, to this day, a decision I have stuck by. Thus church, instead of weekends, was what I lived for at that time.

September came and with it came new challenges and promises. I returned back to Liverpool, into my second academic year of my degree, and all this that had happened wasn't enough to keep me in touch with Jesus. The lifestyle that University offered gave me so much more physical attention and pleasure and it wasn't something I was willing to let go of yet. I think that being a teenager is the most difficult time of our lives. We go from living under our parents to figuring out who we are, what makes us work, and what we are passionate about. We turn so inward to figure these things out. We become selfish and self absorbed, and not because we want everything for ourselves, but because we are trying so hard to figure out who we are alone, who we are apart from our families and parents. We look to different things for identity, attention, and purpose. I got myself in lots of uncomfortable situations, but just thrived in the fact that I was young, free, and careless. I had no responsibility and nothing to hold me back. How silly was I to think that I wasn't about to start learning some of the biggest lessons in life. Hurt people say the most hurtful things thinking that it is going to take away a small bit of pain, replace that small bit of themselves that they feel like they have lost, add that extra brick to the wall they just let down. When actually, all they're doing is buying into the Enemy's schemes, encouraging his influence on their lives, and basically serving a slap up meal for the demon trying, to his best ability, to turn everything back to self and away from God and his love.

I think it is so important to remember that when we give our lives to Christ there is a heart exchange. He takes our broken, sinful, discouraged hearts and replaces them with his perfect beating one. However, just because we switch hearts with Jesus it doesn't mean that all of a sudden we have a free pass at an easy life. It isn't a queue jump. It's a journey like a marathon and not like a sprint. Faith makes things possible not easy.

Jesus was led to the desert by the Holy Spirit to face temptation. If he hadn't have done so, he would not be able to empathise with how difficult we find things. He came and was so very human, he was so very real and emotional and physical. He was born and grew and played and laughed. I find it so difficult to imagine this perfect person as an actual human being. It is so hard sometimes to comprehend that Jesus is the Son of Man. That he came so humbly to the earth. That he created, designed, and spoke into life and lived daily like we live. When he was a child, he would have fallen over and scraped his knees and Mary would have ran over to catch him. He would have learned like we all learned, by reading and doing. He was taught by Joseph how to be a carpenter and do things like cook and clean. And he would have probably had chores to do around the house. He was so very real. So why do we find it so difficult to understand that he can relate to us and that he can empathise with our situations? He has been here and done it, so why do we find it so difficult to go to him?

It should be so much easier for us to fall head over heels in love with someone who can communicate to us, knowing where we are at and what it is that we are feeling. It can be hard to understand that the Bible is not just a collection of stories, it is the LIVING

15

work of God! It isn't just an un-relational collection of accounts about people from a different age that we couldn't possibly draw wisdom from because we are in the 21st century now.

1 In the beginning was the Word, and the Word was with God, and the Word was God. 2 He was with God in the beginning. 3 Through him all things were made; without him nothing was made that has been made. 4 In him was life, and that life was the light of all mankind. 5 The light shines in the darkness, and the darkness has not overcome[a] it.

The Bible is a life-line that God uses to direct us and fill us and encourage us. I think it wasn't until I became passionate about the Bible, and what it was actually telling me on a personal level, that I realised that God is alive right now and that he is speaking directly to me and that he is available to anyone who believes in Christ. It isn't just for particular Christians, it is for us as well. Understand that you don't have to behave like the rest of the people that you see in your church, surrounding, hoping that one day God may give you what he is giving them. What he promises and what he IS is available to you NOW! You do not have to live like the rest of the world and you don't have to look for love in all the wrong places. You can love and be loved by a God who is alive and well!

Grace > The World

CHAPTER 4

Lead me to the cross

T here were multiple things that should have made me trip up into the arms of Jesus. Multiple situations I had faced and overcome. Multiple mistakes I had made and needed forgiveness for. At the age of eighteen, I was very naive in my way of thinking; what life was about, what I should get from it, and where it was leading me. To this day, I wouldn't take back anything that I have done or faced because I know and trust that God has wiped my slate clean and has used those things to make me into the person I am today. I'm a person who can relate to people on many different levels. A person who can use her testing to create this testimony. Something, however, that I do struggle with, and constantly think I have overcome, is forgiving myself. Sometimes it's not about the fact that God can forgive, but that people can forgive. And it's more a question of whether we can forgive ourselves. To this day, I don't think I have forgiven myself for what happened the year I was eighteen. But I can tell you about it and encourage you that if you are facing the spirit of unforgiveness, the last place we often look for it is within. Forgiveness is something that we have to get up every day and consciously choose to do. It is not a onetime event that changes our lives. It is an everyday occurrence that moulds us. It is our free will to forgive and it's something we should be very aware of.

Turning eighteen was a pretty rough year for me even though, in the UK, it is an age we long to turn. It gives us rights legally as a person to be our own person and do whatever we see necessary at that age. It is the legal drinking age for a person here in the UK and that makes life much easier. Being allowed to enter clubs and buy your own alcohol is something the youth of Britain today crave. It is part of our culture and society to enjoy drinking, to, as a teenager, enjoy the club culture. However, my year didn't bring rights and victories, it brought battles and change. This is the year things came to the surface of life that hadn't been there before. This is the year things as I knew them changed, my family as I knew it changed, and this was utterly soul destroying for me. Things changed for me, and at the time I thought it was for the worst, It not only encouraged the hatred I had towards males that I already had developed, but encouraged my miss-trust and miss-use of them altogether. The December before my birthday, I finished a long term 'relationship'. I use this term loosely because it was someone who destroyed my faith in men and my ability to trust someone with my feelings. It was someone who had manipulated, used, and, at the time, came very close to destroying me. This led to a very deep bitterness towards men as a partner, or an equal, and downgraded them in my own little society as something that should be used to satisfy my need as a 'woman'. I tarred all men with the same brush and became my very own Jezebel. This was, however, very common for girls my age and I was no different to those that surrounded me, but that did not make it right. By February, I had a new 'boyfriend' or 'partner', whichever word best suits that of which time with him lasted little. Commitment was now something I feared as controlling, opposed to beautiful, and by the time April came, I had moved onto a different boy. Little did I know, this boy and I would have something in common for the rest of our lives.

Joe and I were in a casual 'relationship', if you could even call it that. This is something that was mass craze in my teen years. Not just for myself, but for the rest of my group of friends, and what I thought the entire population of the world (who also happened to be my age group). Having one person constantly there to go home with at the end of the night-out to satisfy this sexual/emotional/physical need they had developed. That is if someone better didn't arise to spend the lonely hours with; someone to help kill dead time. Well Joe was this person for me, and I for him. At the time, I don't remember having very many feelings for him. Then again, this was just so normal and something I got gratification from, something that was so positively reinforced in my life and group of friends. Neither of us thought we would end up in the position we faced in that June, so when I looked at the pregnancy test that I had hid under my pillow and saw the two lines which indicated that, yes, I was in fact pregnant, I didn't even know how to react. It wasn't something which I had expected. The test was done on a whim, for a reason I don't even remember. Paranoia or to encourage a friend … who knows? The point is, at that moment in time, my worst nightmare had come true. I didn't know who to tell or how to tell them, or what to think, or even how to deal with what was going on in my head. My emotional stability at the time was worse than a boat in the rough sea, and I was having a very hard time processing what was going on in my life.

Obviously, the first person I told was Joe. Out of respect I guess, but that would have been the first time I had expressed that kind of honour. Shortly after, he arrived at my house to talk about our options, like shares in a firm, or plans for a trip. There was no love for this life that God had blessed me with, and an utter disregard to the human being inside me itself. When the decision was made, that I would abort the baby, I thought, at the time, it was the right thing to do. We were both sitting our final A-Levels, both applying to leave for university, both looking for the next best thing in life, craving success, and giving in to the things in life that were fighting for our attention. But a baby was not on the leader-board, and this was deemed, to both of us, as a major setback, which meant that there could only be one option. He did not leave my side throughout the whole of the process and for this I am eternally grateful. To this day, he is someone I hold close to my heart for the way he behaved throughout it all, however grim and awful it may have been. The next person I told was the only person at the time I knew would never leave my side and could help me carry the chains I had tied around my legs. I knew my parents were going through an incredibly difficult time and didn't want to share another burden with them, so of course I went to my God mum, Louise. I remember even when she had him round her house to give him a stern talking to he took it like a man and stuck by my side. He did tell me that the decision was mine and mine alone, but he also reminded me of the plans he had for the future and the plans I had for the future. The way he behaved with me restored some of my trust in man, which ultimately led me to the decision I made. Throughout the whole process my heart wept and to this day it breaks my heart. I often think about what could have been. I don't think I was ever one hundred percent on my decision to disregard life and honour death. And I think this has taken its toll on my healing process. I remember feeling so far away from anyone who understood me. At this point in my life, the only God I had seen had been through my God mum, or at school. I didn't diligently seek him for myself. I didn't even know that I could, or that he even wants me too, but I do remember the heart wrenching disappointment that I knew he must have felt when he realised that I had come to my conclusion. This feeling also welled up in my God mum. She is the person I went to when I realised that I couldn't face it alone. Although I had tried, I couldn't do it. She made every doctor's appointment with me. She held my hand and yelled at those in authority when they were hurting me. I will never forget having a scan in the hospital to see how far along I was and the rage in my God mum's face when the nurse showed me the ultrasound; something I know now was of God, a desperate plea to come to my senses, to realise I didn't really want to do what I was doing, but also a heart destroying realisation for me that I had already made up my mind. Although my God mum never ever yelled at me, or told me she was mad, I knew she was. I knew she was disappointed in the decision I had made, but I knew that she trusted that God had the answer.

It was this trust she had in God that lead me to him the following year. For months and months I had been bitter. Earlier in the year, we had lost siblings of both my best friends at the time. I had to deal with the loss and come to terms with the understanding that God gives as easily as he takes away. But it wasn't seen like that. People were outraged that a girl of sixteen, and an unborn baby, could be taken from this earth before, what we perceived, their time was up. However, through great difficulties come times of immense beauty. And although we may not see it, generations to come will visibly see the legacy left behind by those taken from us too soon. We are so ready to mourn life that is taken from the earth, but what about the life that is alive yet not living?

Anyways, this all hindered my healing process and brought about such a guilt for my irresponsibility. How could I choose to terminate life? A life that I selfishly didn't regard when those who people adored were being taken from us. It broke my heart that during a time of stress I had made a decision I wasn't a hundred percent with, whilst so much more was happening in the world around me. This started the knot of un-forgiveness within me. A knot that, to this day, I am still untying. But it also led me to Jesus. This was the cherry on top of the cake for my decision to allow Jesus to enter my heart, wipe my slate clean, and heal my wounds. This is such an accepted thing in society. Not only terminating life, but dreams, ideas, hopes, and promises. I wouldn't be where I am today without this life event. I know that people suggest this all the time about the things in their past that they cannot change, but sometimes I look back and think I would have been cold hearted and downright rude for a very long time. God had to strip me back, take me to a place where I could have never imagined myself (out of my comfort zone), to wake me up. For this, I am thankful. I struggle with the fact that my heart sings for people and for life, but once, I was a person who had no regard for it what-so-ever. God really does make beautiful things out of dust! Sometimes, I just wish I had that child with me. That I could love and nurture it as I should. As someone who loves me unconditionally. As someone I love unconditionally. I also wonder if they would ever forgive me for the decision that I made. Would they ever see my heart for them and how I yearned for years over someone I had never met and will not meet until I enter my true home. It does give me hope. That one day, I will be able to surround that little human being with love and care and protection. However, knowing that they are with God has to be enough. I often think, *would they have been a boy or a girl? Blonde hair and blue eyes like me maybe?* And although to some of you, this may be a torture of kinds, for me it is an excitement. That this little tiny human being, who is so fragile and delicate, is with God and never had to suffer the things of this world. This is not, by any means, condoning abortion. Anyone who comes to me with the option, it is a simple answer for me now … life! However, it heals my heart to know that God was there to pick up the pieces of my bad choice, and that I caused so much pain and suffering, but he's in heaven looking after my child. Something I could never have done.

As comforting as it is, it does not deal with my unforgiveness. Only time and God will do that. I trust that one day I will be able to look back and not feel the strings in my heart pull with pain. There will be a year when we reach January and I won't think, *oh they would have turned however old this year.* I trust that. That pain will be taken away one day. It may not be whilst I endure life here on earth, but it will happen. I know that there are people out there that have been in my shoes, but there is a bigger plan, a bigger picture that your little jigsaw piece fits into.

God proves daily that he uses this situation to soften my heart. After this decision was made, the thought of being around babies put a fear in me that I didn't want to face. Funnily enough, at the time, one of my close friends had just had a beautiful little girl, Esme. Another had just found out that she was pregnant, and now also has a beautiful little girl, Willow. This was something I found incredibly difficult, and if you ask Charlotte, Willow's mum and one of my oldest friends, it took me a long time to accept the fact that I was dealing with my consequences and had no right to be jealous of her decision, or situation. And that it actually wasn't her fault that she was having a baby, a beautiful little girl that I love very much. But I could not help this allergic feeling I felt when in the presence of a tiny human. This generated over the years until I reached the point where I never wanted kids and I never really wanted to be around them. Obviously, my heart is softening over time. Starting initially with older children and slowly working my way down.

I worked at Camp SWONEKY in 2012 and God used a child below the age of one to 'Woo' me. To encourage the melting of the ice inside my chest. Abigail Grace Carter stole my heart from word go, as with everyone who came into contact with her! My first encounter with her was in a seminar we had to sit in during orientation. My group of friends and I had sat close to the back of the rec hall, which is basically, in simple terms, the staff room. If I am being totally honest, I had checked out before Captain Flanders, the camp director, had started speaking. This was our second year working, and when you have experienced it, you think you know it all. We were the 'cool kids' at camp. Shane and Dawn had been placed at camp this year to work alongside us all and minister in such a kind hearted way. Their daughter, Abby, was only a tiny little baby then. Obviously, everyone had already fallen in love with her cuteness. She has a smile that could make you coo for hours, and such chubby little legs; it was incredibly cute! During the seminar, when I most certainly should have been paying attention, I watched Abby take her first ever steps, and this was like pouring gasoline onto a small, almost extinct flame. My heart sang out with joy! This was such an achievement for her! And to see how proud her parents, Shane and Dawn, were was actually tear jerking. After the seminar, I held her for the first time, of which my friend, Kilein, thought needed photographic evidence. This was the start of my journey into loving God's creation even more, and my regard for the life he blesses us with. I encountered Abby often during camp. In fact, I think I saw her every day for the whole summer. And once the summer had come to an almost close, my 'fear' of being around small children seemed to have disappeared. I enjoyed it more than anything else! I ended up looking after zero to one year olds during a camp session called "Family Camp" and I thoroughly enjoyed it! Luckily, due to having babies surrounding me whilst growing up, and having to be around in the early stages of Esme's and Willow's lives, I kind of had a clue of what I was doing when it came to taking care of them. This was a brilliant help, but it was still tough.

However, all this success came crashing back down when I fell in love. Slowly falling in love with someone who didn't have baggage when the process started, but then all of a sudden has 'baggage' has to be one of the most difficult things I've done. It also doesn't help with my unforgiveness towards myself when surrounded by babies. However, just getting your head around the fact that when you initially started to have feelings for them, you did so on the pretence that circumstances were different and that the hopes you then generated were built on different life factors. I don't know what quite happened for Demichael to get in the situation he did. I have landed the blame a fair few times, of which I suppose could always be an option. If I hadn't have argued with him and pushed him away, if only we were closer, if only we were both less stubborn, who knows. But now, I have a little life who is always going to be a part of my life, irrespective of what happens to me and Demichael. I love this child like my own and I am so blessed to know her and love her. I think when working on our relationship while I was in America, this was the most difficult thing for me. At the time, I constantly put it on the fact that I couldn't bare that he had had his first child with another person. This is a valid reason, but not one big enough to build up resent. I think, in my head, I blamed every reason I could to explain the hurt I felt when I looked at Faith and when I saw him interact with her. I have no reason not to be proud of him. He is absolutely amazing with her. It is a privilege to say that he will be the father of my children because of the care and love that shines from him when he is around

Faith is enough to make any one broody, and I guess I should have said something, but for me, at the time, it wasn't enough. I tried most of the time to block out the fact that he had a beautiful baby. Yeah, it means a lifelong attachment to his ex-girlfriend. You say this could be the reason for the feelings, but it's not. God is working in me, teaching me how to love the unlovable, because sometimes they are the people that need it the most. I am not suggesting that she is unlovable. I know how that statement sounds, but it's not like that. It's hard for a woman to know that her man has had someone else provide a family for him when you know that that is what you were designed to do.

It wasn't until returning to the UK, and speaking with my God mum, that realisation set in. I told her how I was feeling and how I was a little confused that these emotions were bubbling up over the edge with no apparent root that I could find, or even understand. All she did was ask me if I forgave myself. With no other mention of it, I knew exactly what she was talking about, and it pierced me like a knife. To this day, six years on, I still don't one hundred percent forgive myself. And having Faith so close to me, and as a huge part of my life, has ripped the security blanket from my arms. The escape for me was avoidance, and this was my best tactic in my game, but it had now been removed from my deck of cards. This made me feel vulnerable, uneasy, and off guard. So my next tactic was to avoid her. To avoid being around her. This was a miserable fail! How I thought it was going to be pulled off is beyond me! Demichael never once pushed her upon me. He never forced me to do anything I didn't want to do. Although I ask about her every day and absolutely love buying clothes for her and spoiling her in other ways, this will be an ongoing battle for me. I know in my heart that I love her. She is a beautiful, precious creation. Seeing how much Demike loves her makes me love her. She makes him so happy, and in doing so makes me happy. This is a battle I will face for a period of time, of which I have no estimation. It's something God and I have to work on alone. No one will ever take back my decision. Only God can take away the pain and guilt I feel. But I am convinced he has a plan for Faith Marie Nelson, and healing my heart is a part of that.

Give yourself a break, The fact you don't forgive yourself, or even that you feel guilty, should only be a realisation that you are aware of the sin. Take it to God. Lay it at the foot of the cross, because God wants to break that chain.

Grace > Unforgiveness

CHAPTER 5

Fake it til ya make it

1 Peter 3:3-4

"Don't be concerned about the outward beauty of fancy hairstyles, expensive jewelry, or beautiful clothes. 4 You should clothe yourselves instead with the beauty that comes from within, the unfading beauty of a gentle and quiet spirit, which is so precious to God."

Confidence is something I guess we all want. Some of us are blessed with this naturally. For some of us, it comes every now again. Some of us even purchase it from the liquor aisle. The feeling of confidence can come from the thought that you are invincible. Nothing can knock you from your perch. You're against the world and no one can take that feeling from you. For some people, it takes a lot to reach this feeling, and it will come and go with things such as recognition and attention, as well as ability and success. A thing that has a huge impact on this is our feeling of self-worth, how we see ourselves through our eyes, the ones who perceive the cruel world. And that's what it is; a cruel, cruel world. People today are less inclined to accept that humans not only make mistakes, but are very, very different from each other. It isn't very likely that you will meet two people who are identical in every single way. Everyone has different likes, opinions, ideas, talents, and dreams. Perfectionism in this world is too highly regarded. Perfectionism in relationships, perfectionism growing up, etc. Being a teenager can be rough. As rough as the sea in a storm or bark on a tree. It can be cruel just like the world. Starting High School, I was still a nerd who loved books and had little to no regard of my appearance. I didn't do much with my hair or my clothes. It wasn't important to me. I don't suppose it is at that age. That's the least of your worries if you're climbing trees or playing in the garden, making daisy chains and pressing flowers. There seems to be no logic behind getting dressed up. In your first year of high school, this is probably one of the biggest changes you will face. You will start to become interested in makeup and fashion and things that make you feel more grown up. You will even start to look at yourself differently and notice parts of your body you never really knew existed but that you suddenly care about. We all remember this. Self-image is suggested to be an important part of our lives. How we portray ourselves, the style we are more inclined to follow, the colour we dye our hair, the piercings and tattoos we have, the shoes we buy. All these things we chose to make decisions individually. The Enemy will try and destroy you by taunting you about things you yourself can't change, you yourself have no control over. Things you didn't decide to do; such as dye your hair red or wear a short skirt. Things such as your skin colour, the size of your features, and your height. Things that, at the time, you probably would change if you could. In my first year at high school, I managed to fit into a good group of friends. I never really struggled with much. I was always different. I always liked my own things. And luckily, in my first year this didn't change. Being true to yourself, and who you are, is more important than we realise. When people see that you are likely to waver from what you believe in, or what you stand for, they will circle you like vultures until you commit to something not necessarily in the boundaries of your beliefs.

Year eight, aged twelve, a girl from a city around three hours away moved to our school. She was beautiful, skinny, big up top, and as you can imagine, all the boys loved her. This then meant that all the girls wanted to be friends with her. They were fascinated from the stories she brought, being from a different place. Growing up in a small town, you see the same faces day in and day out. Everyone knows more than they should. Thus, when something fresh comes into your life, it can become addictive. She was the addiction. Everyone wanted to be like her. Everyone loved her, and with all due respect, I understood why. I don't blame her for what happened. I also do not resent her in any way for what happened; desperate times call for desperate measures. But for some reason, she had it in for me. I may have been a threat or I may have just rubbed her up the wrong way. Year eight was the year I gave up my self-worth like a balloon to the sky. I fell from what I stood for. I disregarded my beliefs and morals, because all I wanted that year was to fit in, something I don't ever remember wanting before. I wanted to be accepted and apart of a group, and now looking back, it's a blessing that I chose to not fall into that destructive lifestyle of which I led then.

Many of you won't know this, but growing up, I was blonde haired and blue eyed; that appeared to be the problem. I have huge turquoise eyes. They are something some would regard as beautiful. However, for many years, they were a burden, because this was the point of attack. In one year, I went from not even really acknowledging my features to being so conscious of them that it was like I was carrying them in a glass cabinet around with me all the time. I was taunted for something I had no control over. I was ridiculed for having something I did not choose to have. I remember to this day how low it made me feel. It kick started a hatred toward myself that still has a hold on some of the things I do and on the way I look at myself.

People say children can be truthful. They can be so mean and hurtful, more than you would realise. That year, I started cutting myself. I would cut my wrists as a kind of self control. At the time, it was kind of a craze in my school and it appeared so insignificant to everyone, but looking back now so heart breaking. I know I did it for multiple reasons. Attention being one of them, a form of control being the other. I suppose I just wanted my friends to realise that they were hurting me, that they were upsetting me. This year, I lost my true self and found a front, a big mask, that I would wear for the next ten years. I know that this is true to so many girls out there. Girls who would change 'it', whatever 'it' may be. You would rather be anywhere on the planet than where you are now. In fact, even leaving the planet because of 'it' sounds more appealing than what you are going through.

Bullying is not OK! People try and live by the rule that, "only sticks and stones will break your bones, but words will never hurt you." This has to be the falsest statement I will ever read or hear. Physical abuse hurts, but heals much faster than emotional abuse. Emotional abuse shatters you like a mirror and takes much more healing than any other bullying. Walking around school and having people who I respected and regarded as friends shout offensive things at me because I had big eyes was heart shattering and added another ice age to the freezing of my heart. The bullying got so bad this year that I would regularly meet with my head of year. I begged and pleaded for my parents to take me out of school and put me in a different one in a different town. I continued to cut myself and diminished my friendship group to none. I had removed myself from every group of friends I had and convinced myself that I just deserved to be by myself. After a year of a hell I wouldn't want to face again, I decided that I should take a stand for myself. I had built up the walls around my heart, made a mask that I could use to hide the pain and fight the world with ways that should never have been used.

From that day on, I was the life and soul of the party. Alcohol was everyone's best friend. Everyone wanted to get wasted. I managed to fit back into my circle of friends as a boisterous 'up for anything' kind of person, and I let this steal my teen years. Because of this, I grew up too quickly. At the age of thirteen, I had sex. I was in a relationship with a boy a year older than me. Most of my friends had boyfriends and were doing the same. I felt so grown up, like I could take on the world. The front I had formed gave me courage to do things I probably wouldn't have done before, but also with the extra hand from alcohol I was on a roll. We would all save up our dinner money during the week and spend it on our alcohol for the weekend, and we'd get beyond drunk; uncontrollable states. There would be lots of vomit involved, and more than likely blood from fights. To this day, I can say the majority of fights I involved myself in were with males. Apart from two occasions, I have only ever been hit by boys. I have watched people have their faces stamped on and ears bit off because of things I was involved in. These also led to bad choices. Luckily, nothing I ever did hindered my studies. That was something I was, and to this day, am passionate about. But it did tear down a little part of myself, which to this day I'm still building up.

Making bad decisions can often lead to being caught up with other people who make bad decisions, and being away from any kind of hope that you used to hold onto. I lived for the weekend, and wanted everything my own way. I never wanted to miss out on anything that was going on. This led to a breakdown in my relationships with those who cared about me, particularly my parents. They had no control over me or the person I was turning into and I know now that this broke their hearts. It caused many arguments and fights, and often led to me being grounded, which I would often break. I even asked to leave the house and live somewhere else. This wasn't a good thing and often led to weekends drunk. During this time, I formed an awful, even disturbing, relationship with music, of which still has a niggle of control over my life. In time, I know this will dissolve, but whenever I listen to a particular type of music, the rush comes. The need for alcohol rises up inside of me and takes ahold of my insides and rattles me. This is huge within our culture. People are so controlled by music, it is insane! This control almost destroyed my life. When I was fifteen years old, I made a decision whilst under the influence of alcohol which could have had irreplaceable repercussions. I remember the night like it was yesterday. I had been out drinking with my friends for probably the second night in a row. I had returned home after an argument with a very close friend at the time, which ended in me smashing up her phone. Running into my house, in a drunken stupor, the consequences of my state had been displaced in my mind due to the events that had previously happened. However, they had not slipped from the memory of my parents. They were both sitting there waiting for me; bearing in mind that I was probably in much later than had been agreed. I watched the rage cross my dad's face, although I probably couldn't see too straight myself. In films, they depict rage with steam coming from people's' ears. Well, I now understand. He was so cross with me and with the lack of control he had on his daughter, who was spiralling out of control. Now although I have no children of my own, I understand how it must have felt to be so disappointed in someone's behaviour, and not being a big enough impact to change things. My friend had followed me home, probably hoping to sort things out, not realising what she was about to get herself involved in. My dad lost his temper that night. I was totally a spoiled brat about it all and after a very heated row, and a very upset mother, I ran off with my friend, with no plan of going back home. After calming down and sobering up (it must have been early hours) I decided that the warmth of my own bed was much better than a park bench, or wherever else I could have ended up, so I went home. This wasn't the only reason I went home. I went home because that night, I wanted to die. I wanted to remove myself from the hurt, from the brokenness of the world, from the life I led. I wanted to fix things myself. However little did I know that as a human being without Jesus, I have little to no control. I entered my house and went straight for the cupboard, which I knew contained pills, and collected every box I could find. Luckily, it wasn't common for us to have a lot of medicine stored in the house. I filled a flask full of alcohol. I remember sitting there and taking every single pill that I had and drinking the last drops of liquid, and then climbing into bed, hoping never to open my eyes again. It actually blows my mind now to see how I should not have woken up from that. How my time here should have been over. God had a different plan for me that night, and it fills me with so much love and joy to know that even when I didn't know him, he knew me. And he protected me. In the early hours of that morning, I woke myself up vomiting. I had already vomited in my sleep and was incredibly lucky to not have choked. The feel of regret and dread that I then felt was so overwhelming, I didn't know what to do. I knew I had to get up and get someone, to get help, but the vomiting was uncontrollable. I remember crawling to the toilet crying and screaming through the sickness. This woke my parents. My dad must have had enough and had sent my mum down to see what was going on. My mum has to have one of the softest hearts I have ever known and has unconditionally loved me and my brother since the day we were both born, This often meant she couldn't stay mad at us for long. Seeing me in this state, she looked distressed. She sat on the side of the bath and said to me, "Oh Sam, what a mess. Are you okay?"

There and then I couldn't get my words out quick enough. From that point on, the following events are a blur. I know she woke my dad in panic. Everything happened so fast. I remember my dad calling an ambulance. I remember how quickly it felt like it came. I remember laying in the back of the ambulance, not quite knowing what was going on or how I felt, or what I had actually done. But I do remember seeing my dad sitting next to me crying. This had to be the first time I had ever seen my dad cry, and it was because of something I had done. Because of a very silly decision I decided to make. I don't remember getting to the hospital. I do remember being asked so many questions. I don't remember what happened to me in the hospital or who visited me, or even how long I was there. I do remember my parents and brother never leaving my side. Not once did my dad leave. I don't even remember him taking time out to go to the restroom. However, those days were such a blur.

I was incredibly blessed to just leave that hospital alive, with merely a psychiatric referral and not someone else's liver. This did not kick start me into a realisation of where I was and what I was doing was wrong, but it was the last time I ever tried to kill myself. And it was the last time I ever cut my wrists.

It did make me realise what I wanted from life. Speaking to a psychologist really intrigued me. After a few referrals, I was deemed mentally safe and I returned to the normality of life. This isn't an event in my life that I choose to review very often. I don't like the decisions I made and I have watched people make really bad decisions. I have made really bad decisions and these have all been forgiven by God's saving grace. Looking back at the person I was throughout my time at school, I am lucky to say I escaped. I escaped the cage of self-destruction that the Enemy places over us encouraging us to think we cannot get out, we cannot see mercy. God picked me before the world was even created to be holy; a crucial member of the church, a person whose past is forgiven and wiped clean, and all the glory really does belong to him. What I have realised is that I am not the only teenager to have suffered the way I did during my time at school. The result of my actions, or other people's actions, could have taken my life from me and from my family. People need to realise how much they are loved, and that the only person they should have courage in is God. Because we can do all things through Christ who strengthens us. Teenagers are so vulnerable, to the point where things that happen can affect these children for the rest of their lives. It could have an effect on their destiny. They are tarred with such a callous brush by the perfectionists in society when all they really need is love. God's love. Those hardest to love need it the most, and I can tell you right now that the teenagers on the streets today need our love. They need to know God. Luckily, during my school years, I didn't really encounter drugs. When I did, I had my head screwed on enough to make an educated decision on if I wanted to take part in that rebellion; although this sense didn't last long. Just because I escaped death, it doesn't mean the demons that I fought during those years of self-loathing had disappeared. Yes, they had subsided, but I can tell you now that unless you deal with the root of something like that, it will rear its great big dirty head again until you deal with it, until you take it to the foot of the cross and offer it to God, declaring you can't face it alone. God doesn't look at us and see the imperfect versions of ourselves we see. As humans, we are so disposed to view our faults over the beauties that we have. We let these faults drag us down, we let them define us, we let them determine the person we are. When in reality, if we focused on the positives and saw ourselves like our Father does, then it would be unlikely for us to deal with things such as bulimia. Fighting body image issues is likely for us all. Everyone has something they wish they could change. However, they probably go a sensible way about it. Eating disorders are more common than people think, and can easily be covered up with something else. From someone else's perspective, an eating disorder can be the stupidest thing they have ever heard. However, to someone who despises the way they look, it's the only answer. I don't remember when I started making myself vomit. I don't even remember why or for what reason, but I do remember the lengths I would go to to cover it up, to prevent someone from thinking it. Living with my best friend Kelsey made this increasingly difficult. I think for the majority of the time, she knew what was going on. Bearing in mind that it was part of our degree to be able to read the signs of psychological dispositions. Anyways, this was a part of my life up until very recently, when I think I realised what was going on. When I realised how stupid I was being. I realised who I should have courage in, who loves me, who strengthens me and upholds me, who I love, and who I want to be. It wasn't until I realised these things that I realised what I was doing to myself, and how stupid it was. But at the time, I thought it was so right, and the best thing for me to do. Self-worth is a bit like a heart; only God can fix and fill it fully, but we try and do it ourselves with the ways of the world, We don't realise how delicate and important it is. It is only when we value ourselves that we can value our creator, and in turn, the works he does through us. Without loving ourselves, it can be increasingly difficult to love people, as well as the love they feel for us. We can't see what they see and we don't feel worthy. I recently had an argument with Demichael, not to air our dirty laundry, but to get across the point that every single person on this planet deserves to be loved by other people on the planet and even undeservingly by our heavenly father. I had mentioned something to him, probably something about going on a diet or not being happy about the way I looked, and had been so confused at how he could look at me and be attracted to me. This really frustrated him, and I had no clue why. It had caused an argument because he couldn't see what I see. But in reality, all he wanted me to know was that it doesn't matter what I see, because what he sees he Loves. All of it. He thinks all of me is beautiful. Even crazy me! In his temper, he said, "Ok, for now I give up, but when you realise that I love everything about you, and nothing will change that, let me know." Although he hadn't given up, and it was very apparent that he was just waiting for me to stop acting crazy, it made me think about God. How God puts up with so much of our crazy because we feel so inadequate, when in reality, he is saying exactly the same as Demichael, "Look, I love all of you. Even your deepest darkest secrets. I love you so much that I want to help change you. I want to help you grow and turn away from those things in life that have ahold of you." That kind of love can't be found anywhere here on earth and it led me to 1 Peter 3:3-4. How we look to God means nothing. He doesn't care if our hair is frizzy or we think we look dreadful without make up, or we're too fat or too skinny, or don't wear the smartest clothes. That is something society has set as a standard. Something that the world rules over, not God. What he finds beautiful is our gentle hearts, and that is great worth to God. It really is about what is on the inside. We all carry our own crosses. Each person has a different cross that they have to wake up and carry each day. That they have to leave outside the office door or outside the betting shop door. That they leave in the street whilst they slope off down a backstreet to meet their dealer. That they leave in bed as they wake up to feed their baby in the night. Each one of us has a cross to carry. What person can understand this more than Jesus? He gets it. He carried his own cross. All the way to the place where he would be nailed to it. Jesus carried this cross so that we would not be plagued with the worry about tomorrow. So that we no longer have to live by law, but by the spirit that has been sent to dwell in us. When we decided that we love Jesus, the word tells us that we are also crucified with Christ and that we no longer live for us, or by ourselves, but Christ lives in us, and we live for him, and with him daily. The life I live in the body, I live by faith in the son of God who *loves* me and gave his life for me. Not just me, but for each person on the planet that has been and is to come.

Grace > Our Issues

CHAPTER 6

Hail SWONEKY

I don't think I quite realised how much deciding to go to America for the summer would change my life in every way possible. I just wanted to leave behind the troubles of yesterday and do something new and different for a few months. It was never intended to take over or have high impact, just a bit of fun. However, I met people there that have impacted my life more than you can ever imagine. Some of the most important people in my life, I met in America at summer camp. Typical right?

Camp is the battle field. You are literally front line fighting. It is incredible! You make friends with people here in a way that is not possible in the normal world. The children that come to camp are inner-city children who are often from neglected, abusive, or foster homes. Thus you find yourself in some very, very tough situations that you literally couldn't even comprehend. It can be so heart breaking to love on people knowing it may be the first time they have ever seen love. It's also challenging to discipline these kids that have come from no routine, discipline, or even understanding of what is wrong and right.

Days at camp are long. Let me tell you a bit about the days there and you can decipher for yourself how intense you think this is. Firstly, the Senior Counsellor will wake everyone in the cabin to get up and ready for flag rising. The age group determines how easy this task can be, regardless of which, each age has its difficulties. After flag rising, everyone will attend breakfast as a whole camp. The job here is to assist and supervise the children in getting their food and cleaning up after themselves. After this, everyone will return back to the cabin where the children will clean up their own personal areas. Yes, you read that correct. We make the campers clean up after themselves. Some may call it torture, some discipline. I personally feel sorry for the counsellors who have to endure the countless moans and fights and tears that accompany this part of the day. Then the whole camp returns together to worship together in Chamberlin Hall, and learn new bible stories and lessons about Jesus. The counsellor's role here is to encourage the children to get involved and also to supervise, but if we are being honest, their real role here is to let out their inner child. Children attend clubs after morning worship. In this time, counsellors lead an activity or find themselves with spare time to complete paperwork, because there are countless numbers of incident reports for you to do. Paperwork at camp is an essential mandatory part of the day. Because we work with at risk children, everything needs to be documented to ensure the safety of each child. Lunch then occurs. After lunch, the children will swim. This was always my favourite part of the day. I always made sure that I was on for pool. One pro is that it's a brill time to see your Lifeguard friends (the Machados in particular). Let me tell you about these beautiful women of God. They are all three inspiring in their own ways. They all encourage and love on me. I cannot imagine my life without their friendships now. The miles between us have not separated us in the slightest; how amazing is technology! Alyssa has been such a mentor to me. She has helped shape me and pointed me in God's direction almost literally every day. Another pro of the pool is that you get to top up your tan. After this, each cabin attends a program activity on the campground. An example would be riding horses or going on a trek into the wilderness, or even visiting the farm. Next, it's time for Dinner. I would say this is the craziest part of the day. It's really hot by this time and the kids are agitated. There has been enough time for drama to brew, and it's usually a changeover of staff at this point, so you are absolutely dying for a break if you have been on all day. After dinner, children will have free time to burn off steam. It is the counsellor's job to make decisions as to what their cabin will do. Usually an activity as a cabin is necessary to take them away from everyone and restore a little calm to the day, but the likelihood is that they will want to either go and ester the boy campers, if they are in the older cabins, or run riot on the playground. After free time, an evening program for the entire camp is attended. This could be anything from sitting and watching a play to orienteering as a whole camp, and other such things. Honestly, depending on what activity, this would be my favourite part of the day. One year, we did a superhero hunt and things got wild. It was literally a bit like the purge; just absolute carnage! Campers vs. Staff; oh happy days! Throughout the day, the senior counsellor has to manage 20+ campers and 3 staff members under them. They have to work as part of a team to ensure the children have as much safe fun as possible, so things can be pretty manic in that position; not forgetting that days can sometimes be 24 hours. Before bedtime, each cabin will take part in a devotion devised by the counsellors of that cabin. This is usually another bible teaching and a reflection on the day which is perfect opportunity to wind down before bed, but also to talk about Jesus and what they have, or haven't learned. Bedtime also comes with lots of structure. Showers and free time are before lights out. Otherwise, you are asking for trouble; especially with the older cabins. The counsellor's' job doesn't finish there however. Paperwork for the day is to be completed and usually a cabin meeting will be held before staff bedtime. A lot of the time, staff will leave camp to get food that isn't quite as disgusting as camps but probably more calorific. A senior counsellor's job is very demanding yet very rewarding. Tired yet? Well that was an example of a stress free day.

During my time at camp, I learnt more skills than I can list. I learnt how to work as part of a leadership team and how to manage people within my team. I learnt more about myself than any other time in my life. I learnt what I want from life and what I want to provide. I learnt how to love, to love the people I work with, to love the people I work for, and to love the children I see day in-day out, regardless of the circumstance. Management at Camp is very well respected and serves the children and staff to the best of their ability. My co-counsellors worked year in-year out to the best of their ability and I couldn't have asked for a better staff force. The hardest part of the job is seeing broken children, but everything after that is rewarding. Knowing that you're making a difference in their lives, removing them from abusive, neglectful, poverty ridden homes, is all you need to be reminded to find the strength to face the long days. It's also incredibly difficult to leave behind the relationships that you have made. These people you work with, cry with, face challenges with, and laugh with in such intense situations day in and day out become family.

My very first week at camp was one of the most challenging weeks of my life. I think up to this point I didn't really know what I was actually even doing at camp. I didn't particularly like America and I especially didn't like children all that much, but there was a little girl in my cabin that year that changed my heart more than I ever thought was possible. Her story is one of the most tragic ones I know. I am not going to go into detail, but I do want you to know how amazing she is and how I thought about her every day for the rest of the summer. I literally could not have emotionally gotten through that week if it wasn't for the amazing counsel of my co-workers and my boss, Angela. Angela has to be one of the softest spirits I've met, but she is totally a diva for Jesus, and this was my first real encounter of a woman who was sold out for God. At the time, I totally didn't understand what was so attractive about who she was, but now when I look back, the fact that she knew exactly who she was in Christ was exactly what it was.

Camp will always be my second home and a piece of my heart always there. When I look at my life now, it is a product of that encounter. With incredible people like Amy and Jerome, who have impacted and continue to impact my life daily. I continually get blown away by their love for me. How they serve me and encourage me. How they always have my back. Friends like that can only be made at a place like Camp SWONEKY. They're not friends for me anymore, they are my family. It is where I found myself and it is where I found Jesus. As well as those I now call my family. It has a special place in this book to be honoured in my journey, and for all those people out there who think that Camp is an easy summer situation; it is not! It is the front line. All of the above that I have described to you is behind enemy lines. It is up front and personal and it's the infantry of the army of God. It is tough and it is challenging, but most importantly, it is full of Growth, Freedom, and Breakthrough.

Grace > The Challenge

CHAPTER 7

Cupid's Lair

C amp is easily like Cupid's Lair. That companionship of someone who shows you love and affection whilst we battle the Enemy day in-day out seems to be of some comfort to us throughout the scorch of the summer months. It's so easy to be 'in love' with your summer fling. I think most of you will join me when saying a summer fling very usually stays in the summer, hence the term. Everyone is so caught up in the laughing, fun, change, freedom, and especially the beautiful weather, that they don't think rationally, or so I thought. In fact, my first year at SWONEKY, I was positive that the sun made people deluded. My first year, I was still a 'sponge follower'. This is a term I used to describe people who just soak up Jesus but don't actually pour out. I hadn't yet fallen in love with Christ. However, what did happen my first year did kick-start the domino effect which lit the fires of my heart and started to melt the deepest darkest corners of my soul. Very few people make it back out past the gates of cupid's lair, because that means real world effort. Camp is like a completely different world of which you cannot explain until you experience it yourself. It is, for me, very much like the elixir of life; a life line, one you can't let go. The real test is when everyone goes home to reality, to school and jobs. This is where the real test is. The cost vs. benefit weighing scales are pulled from people's rational minds and emotions often get over-looked like last week's mail. The hassle of working on something like a relationship is, in this day and age, too much effort. People today would much rather quit. I am sometimes one of them. Sometimes, I just want to hold my hands up and say, "OK, you win!" However, I have come to realise that if you can't fight for love, what can you fight for? I often think of how our grandparent's generation managed to make it so many years together. What was it? Did they live in a time where a different kind of love lived? Was there a secret passed on from generation to generation about how to keep love alive? Then I realised that in those days, they fixed things that were broken, and they didn't discard them as out of use. My Granddad was a fixer, and if I think about it, my Nanna is quite the same. Nothing is of no use; everything can be fixed, or adapted in being used for something. In my case, it wasn't just the fact that we had both gone home and back to reality, with the possibility of meeting up every now and again. Oh no, I wasn't that intelligent!

I did find myself caught up in an unintentional end of summer fling. It was kept on the down low because I wasn't a big lover of love and didn't want people to know that I had been knocked off my feet. Regardless, there is a dirty big ocean in between me and my 'summer fling', which made me discard my emotions and let 'rational' set in! Being able to wait is a sign of true love and patience. If you can wait for that one person then that is true declaration of your love for them. Anyone can say, "I love you," but not everyone can wait around and prove that it's true. In fact, it is easy to say those words. They often hold a very different meaning in today's society. A meaning with less weight and commitment attached to them. Often, when I think of love I think of … well God, yes … but I also go back to my favourite Bible verse, 1 Corinthians 13:4-8.

"Love is patient. Love is kind. It does not envy. It does not boast. It is not rude. It is not self-seeking. It is not easily angered. It keeps no records of wrongs. Love does not delight in evil, but rejoices with the truth. It always protects, always trusts, always hopes, always perseveres. Love never fails."

I know first-hand being able to do all of these is so difficult. Jeesh is it difficult! We as humans have set such a high bar for the standard of love. How we should lavish our loved ones with gifts. How we should only be able to spend our lives with someone with an amazing job and no baggage. Or someone who takes you away every other weekend. How chivalry is dead, and other such things. People who we put on a pedestal and respect as role-models (particularly 'A-listers') set such a bad standard of love. People suggest that there is a line that is drawn in a relationship and when the other person crosses it, that is every excuse to pack up and leave like a bird migrating for winter. We need to take it right back to the very first line. The very first descriptor of love. The very first indicator of how we should love …

"Love is patient." Understanding this helps us to realise that we do not discard love when it doesn't work exactly how we want it to. We don't discard it and find a new one. Love is actually a daily conscious decision. When we add boundaries to things, we limit our patience. We put a ticking clock on how long it will be until we snap like an elastic band. Ultimately, we put God in a box. What do we believe God for in the realm of loving people? It took personal experience for me to experience this.

"Excellence is the result of caring more than others think is wise, risking more than others think is safe, dreaming more than others think is practical, and expecting more than others think is possible."

I used to be a firm believer in a relationship being fifty-fifty. It takes two to tango, and all that. I guess this relieves some of the pressure to perform, giving you a break every now and again. To not particularly care. This, I no longer believe to be true. A relationship is never fifty-fifty. It should always be one hundred-one hundred. However, in life that's not always possible. Sometimes in life, the person we love may not be where they want to be. They may be dealing with hardship, or loss, or trials that you are not facing. And this causes the relationship to become forty-sixty, thirty-seventy, and so on. This doesn't mean that you should use this as an indicator of when your patience should run out. It does, however, mean that sometimes you have to carry the one you love. To protect and support them. And it isn't always butterflies and rainbows. Also, you don't always get what you want. But isn't that like the love of God? I am not suggesting that God sometimes can't love us one hundred percent, because he is always more than capable of loving us more than we could ever imagine. But if we can't see God's love in our partner, then where can we see it? God relentlessly is in love with us.

My walk with Demichael is nothing but rocky. However, I don't resent it. And I wouldn't take back a single moment. It has been almost five years since I met him. He will insistently tell you the date of our anniversary was June 6th, 2011 (the day we first met). At first, I could not stand to be in the same vicinity as him. He just rubbed me up the wrong way. There was actually not a reasonable explanation for why he annoyed me so much. A defence mechanism maybe? God only knows. For an entire two months, I worked alongside him. And for two months, I avoided him. I had seen boys like him before. I had dated boys like him before. Ladies' boys. Yeah, I knew the type very well. And that was just another excuse to avoid him like the plague, which I did successfully. I don't know if I have mentioned, but my original reason to go to camp was to get over an 'ex-boyfriend', or 'love interest', however you want to describe it. Someone who I had recently split from. Thus the thought of having anything with any kind of male revolted me. And I was never the 'lovey dovey' type to begin with. As far as I am concerned, God had different plans for me and my heart of stone.

My first positive encounter with Demichael Lewis Nelson was after camp had finished. Now this is a sad affair, because looking back, I would have loved to have spent the whole summer getting to know him better. However, the weeks I did spend with him are irreplaceable, and have had a long-term effect, not only on the way I think and treat people, but my heart itself.

Leaving for the UK after my first summer fling was difficult. I do remember crying on the plane and then asking myself what on earth had happened over summer. I spent the nine hours reflecting on myself and my situation, although this was still not a solid enough foundation for my love of Christ to take over my life like the tide over the shore. Still being caught up in the emotions of the summer, I think at one point we decided that we would 'date'. Both of us still being very immature, this didn't last long and one little argument meant we didn't speak for the month of December. Therefore, we decided it was best to give up and not fix things. At this point, I was caught up in my final year of university, and the trials and parties that it brought. So I didn't pay much attention to him. We did occasionally speak, but it wasn't until around my birthday that we started speaking again. When I realised God was calling me back to camp and let him know, things were soon rekindled. We relit the fire that burnt so bright when we were together at camp. We connected again. We spoke on Skype. We spoke on the phone. It was lovely to speak again, but he was never the person I knew over the phone or the internet. He wasn't the person I had connected so much with at camp. I didn't know the reasons why, and my first night back in America came as bitter sweet. It was so good to be back with my family, with the people I love more than anything. And the thought of seeing Demichael brought such a joy to my heart. It gave me a little bit more of a purpose. I was scared of being vulnerable, I was, but it didn't matter. I just wanted to see him and spend time with him. However, things this summer were going to be very, very different. I found out on that first night of camp 2012 that Demike was expecting a baby to a girl he was potentially dating. Crushed is one word I would use to describe this. Devastated is another. I tried my best to hide it, and I think to everyone but my camp brothers I did. Kemar and Napa however, can see through any front I try and put on, and they always made it very apparent that they were with me whatever happened. To this day, I know that to be true. They are both the craziest people I will ever come across, but I know, more than anything, that they will *always* have my back. That summer, we had our ups and downs, or pros and cons. We hurt each other, and other people in the process. We fought like cats and dogs. But secretly, (well I say secretly, but it's not a secret if Deairra, Demichael's little sister, knows), but secretly, all I wanted was him. Was for the Demike I knew. And no matter how much I denied it, for the Demike I loved to come back from wherever he was hiding. From whatever cave or pit or stone he was under and live in the amazing person he really was. I saw a different side to him that summer. A side I didn't particularly like. But then again, I showed a different side to me that summer. A side I didn't like. Although I spent my graduation with him, and of course my amazing camp family, I didn't like the people we had turned each other into. So I decided that I no longer wanted to be a part of whatever messed up relationship we had. What a mess!

It took months for him to eventually tell me, himself, the situation he was in; which was just another firm indicator to me that this was someone I didn't know or like any more. I longed for the Demichael I knew. The 'Cheese Ball' who would act like a fool because he's scared of everything. The guy who told me things about his life even though he didn't particularly know me. Who would have a joke with me and be there for me to hold me and kiss me like no one else ever had. So there and then, I threw in the towel. I was certain that he was in there somewhere, but I wasn't about to wait around and find out for myself. I mean it's not like we had known each other all that long. We had spent literally a month together. But it was as if we had known each other for years. I don't know if it was because we could be vulnerable with each other on a different level than with other people. I remember one night, after our second cinema date, Demike spilled his little life story to me and it blew me away. Not because of how powerful it is, but because he felt like he could open up to me like that. He was the kind of person who just kept himself to himself and was quite mysterious actually. You only ever got surface level Demike. However, that night it got deep, and he opened up to me. And then a racoon appeared on the porch and that book snapped shut! Looking back, that night we shared a part of each other that no one had before. It was powerful.

Coincidentally, the day his beautiful baby girl, Faith Marie, was born, I happened to be at his house collecting his sister. He was happy. I hadn't seen this for a while, but that day, I did see a glimpse of his old self. However, it didn't last long. It faded like a shadow into the light. I didn't see him again. I thought that would be the last time I ever saw him, and from that day on I was moving on. Whatever these feelings were that I was feeling then were false. I knew best. I had a better plan. I had lost him and I had to force myself to let it go. God, however, probably laughed at me right there and then in his heavenly throne. I don't even think it was a week later when the news that Demike and his friend JR were coming back to camp to visit. My heart SANK instantly. How was I ever supposed to 'get over' someone who I had to constantly see? I didn't want to let anyone in on the fact that I was so disheartened by their return. That night, however, kept the fire burning in my heart. The walls were coming down! At the time, I was absolutely devastated, because I knew I had never felt like this about anyone before. I know it was something that I fought for for a long time, but the reality was that I was scared. I didn't know how to deal with the emotions that I was feeling. I was slightly excited that a light I had never seen before was lighting up and starting to glow brighter and brighter.

That night was a gift from God. Purely, innocently a gift from our Heavenly father. There is no doubt in my mind about that. Astonishingly (I say this with slight sarcasm because we all know that God's plan is much better than our own) there was a meteorite shower that night. We spent our night laying on the bench by the lake, watching the clumps of space burn up in the earth's atmosphere. Space that was ordinary but found its end so extraordinarily, in the earth's protective layers. This was the first time he had seen a shooting star. That night, he was resuscitated. I was resuscitated. Back into realisation of what God is and what he has planned. That night, I never want to forget. That night, I wrote about, in so much detail, in my journal. I just had to get all these emotions down on paper. That night, I did one more thing; I allowed myself to fall in love. Although it was something I knew was about to come to an end again, (I was to go travelling the States and then return to the UK, and I were never to see him again), I couldn't help it. I also underestimated the power of God. A week later, Demike and JR were back at camp Working!

For my situation today, I will forever blame Eguie Machado. You, kind sir, let God rule through your heart. No matter how much I tried to convince you it was a bad idea for the boys to come back and work at camp, you also decided that it might be a good idea to put me in charge; particularly of Demike and JR. Although I did contest a little, I didn't want to give away anything, so from that day on, I supervised the boys All the while, fighting the fact that I was head over heels in love with one of them I was trying my best to, not only hide it, but deny it to everyone, including myself, and to be professional. Although we thought we knew our indefinite destiny of going back home, back came the gates of cupid's lair approaching fast, so we seized the moment. I don't think I spent much time with anyone but him. The person I had been yearning for was back. I don't remember being much happier. The walls were still melting like Narnia! I am sure to this day that God was using Demike to transform my heart. To give me new life. To help me find my saviour. He may not be the reason I fell in love with Jesus, but he did have a severe storm impact. I still had, however, convinced myself that this was the end and that God was blessing us with time together because it was unlikely that we would see each other again. I did actually have no control over my feelings at that moment in time. And although I didn't admit it to myself, or anyone around me, I was surely falling deeper and deeper in love. Like an avalanche down a mountainside. It was happening and there was no stopping it. No stopping it at all. I said goodbye to Demike when I left for Chicago with my friends, Fran and Sarah, to meet my friend Kelsey. It was as hard as I thought it was going to be! Regardless of which, I had to hold it together. That morning, he wrote in my journal and left his angry birds (angry bird due to my camp nickname) t-shirt, which he had also wrote a note on, on my bed. I spent the whole journey to Columbus, OH with that t-shirt on my lap. Clinging on for dear life. Like if I let go, I would lose a part of myself. I tried my best to not let it effect my time with my friends, Sarah and Mary, because I wasn't just leaving Demike and America, I was leaving some of the most important people in my life who helped shaped who I was becoming, and who always loved on me and always forgave me.

Fran, my beautiful heavenly sister, knew it hurt, and I knew the hurt she was feeling. I didn't like owning up to things like this, it was severely out of character for the person I was then, but inside it was all falling apart.

Winona Lake has to be one of the most beautiful places I think I will ever visit. It is so tranquil, quaint, and homely. Fran and I both adored the place. It was lovely to spend time away from the intensity of camp and the emotions. As well as just spending time together as sisters. I am so blessed to have these people in my life. They offer such wisdom and hope. Fran, that day, on a beach in Winona Lake, offered me much, much more.

"If you want to know where your heart lies, look to where your mind wanders," is the quote that came out of her mouth that day and offered a big reality check. Another big slap in the face. A big, "Hello, are you stupid?" So what was it that my mind wandered to? You bet ya it was … Demike. My mind didn't just wander, it went there and stayed there for hours on end. I wanted to let him know, but just didn't know how. I'd never told anyone before how I felt about them, because I had never had real feelings for them. I don't believe you should tell people things to please them. How would I even begin to tell him? I didn't even know how I was feeling, never mind have the ability to explain it! So I wrote him a letter which looked a little like this:

"Hope is believing there's a chance, a chance of something better, a better future a chance to prove yourself to world, a chance to be the person you want to be, a chance that one day things will change, although with hope comes courage, courage is taking those first steps to your dream even if you cannot see the path ahead. Nothing good comes easily you will lose the things you thought you loved, give up the things you thought you needed but suffering acquires character and strengthens us to do great work, no one is going to make our dreams come true and it is your own job to get up every day and work toward the things deepest in your heart, I'm doing all this in faith because God is good. I love you."

I didn't even know how I was going to get it to him, but I knew that I had to: A) Get it down on paper. And B) At least try. I don't know if you've ever had an idea that, at the time, is amazing, but after you have slept on it, your balloon pops. Well this is how I felt, and I had started to convince myself that it was a bad idea and that I shouldn't show my feelings. But then there was a change of events that meant I had to unlock my heart. After the realisation that God wanted me to stay in America, I had to let him know. This gave us hope. God plants something in your spirit and sometimes you just cannot let it go. Well this was one for me, and for a long time, even now, I battle with my heart about what happens being from God and not my heart. But that was from God.

Just because I had come to this realisation did not mean for one second that things were, or are, going to be easy. They, in fact, became more difficult than I realised. We both have baggage. You could say him a little more than me. But his baggage is beautiful. And it stole my heart the day I first saw her, although I tried to fight it, just like everything else. It took awhile for us to both realise what we wanted, even after we realised we were in love. And sadly, a lot of people were hurt in the process, and for this I am sincerely, eternally sorry. God took me to the West Side Salvation Army in Cincinnati, Ohio to fall in love with Him. To learn more about him and his nature. To give me His dream for my life. People think that I went there for Demike. I know that. I am not stupid. But if only you knew what was going on in the other dimensions. I also was put there to love each and every single one of the people there. One of the people I met there has had more of an impact on my life than she will ever know. I have managed to tell her this previously, but I am convinced she is an angel from heaven. Though God teaches us how to love wholeheartedly, she has been my earthly example that I will always follow by, and if I end up half the woman of God she is, I would be incredibly proud of myself.

God gave me a dream that I know will come to pass. That I know he has been setting me up for in the past few years, There will be life spoken into the dry bones of Price Hill.

This woman took role as Demichael's spiritual mother for the majority of the time she has been in West Side. This woman is as important, if not as, to him as his own mother. The opinion of this woman, therefore, is highly regarded in every aspect of both of our lives now. However, at the time, I was more worried about how she would accept me than what she thought of our relationship. I wanted nothing more than for the people important to Demichael to like me. Anyways, my main focus was Jesus. This is the point in my life where I realised that Jesus was my shining star. My one and only. My counsellor. My hope and saviour. And my prince of peace. I wanted her to see Jesus in me. I wanted her to see Jesus' love pour out of me.

So waiting for the right moment to tell Captain Kim was crucial. We had managed to keep it secret for so long. Even though Jerome, my big brother and youth pastor at west side, had been there every step of the way into the relationship, she happened to be 'clueless'. I am convinced everyone had been talking, or that she must have had an idea. Captains' campfire was a highlight of my time in west side, and I do hope to endure many more awful scary stories and laugh until I cry at how the boys torment Captain in love. This one particular campfire, however, took a turn I didn't expect. After a stern word with Demike in the Kitchen about telling people before they found out from other people, he took this maybe a little too literal and darted outside to where everyone was gathered. I had no clue what was going on but felt the burning of eyes on me. I looked up and stopped breathing straight away. I knew what had happened. I knew what he had done and I was shocked. I didn't quite know how to react or what to say or do. Although I was so scared, God has blessed us with an amazing understanding, caring, loving captain that wants nothing but the best for all of us, and who happily gave her blessing. There and then, I felt accepted. Not just as Demike's girlfriend, but as part of the family. I felt good enough. I felt like she could see Jesus in me, and I was bursting with joy!

"The desire to reach for the stars is ambitious; the desire to reach hearts is wise." – Maya Angelou

Grace > Acceptance

CHAPTER 8

Significant Me

K ites look better when you stand and watch them float in the sky. They look so majestic floating on the wings of time, hovering above all the earth, watching over everyone. They are a great marvel as they stay hovering so high, with little to no effort at all. If you just stand and watch the beautifulness of what's happening above, you, and everyone, can see them that way. However, if you choose to grab them and run, as we often do, it's likely that they will break. If not, they will more than likely sink low, so people will not really be able to see the beautifulness of a kite floating in the sky, and it will lose its splendour and glory, being dragged behind, pushing against the winds of life. Remind you of something? It makes me think of my life. Sometimes, I just wake up thinking, *Today, I am grabbing life and running. I am running as far as I can, as fast as I can, and I am going to do this!* But in reality, if we wait, if we take it one day at a time, one beautiful moment of God-blessed life at a time, we too float like Kites in the sky for all to see; with such ease and elegance. This is what catches people's eyes. They wonder why we can face life in such a way. They want to know. They want what we have. This is such a gift from God, that if we live each day for him, in love, it catches people's attention more than fireworks in the sky. This is how I want to live. I want people to look at me and ask what I have that they don't, and I want that to be Jesus. I was recently talking to a friend who was facing some troubles, and she asked me how I could be so positive all the time. I laughed in her face! Positive me? You have got to be joking! I felt like I constantly moaned to God about my hardship, about how things were not fair and how I wanted them to change. And I did. So badly! I felt like I was cut off from the world. It was the 'Great Wait', but I still lived Loving God although it was hard. She told me I always had a positive outlook and it was something she loved about me. This was such a compliment, but I didn't want her to think that just because I tried to live in faith that everything was easy for me, because it wasn't. So I told her that I am like every other person on the planet with or without God, going to face trials. I am negative at times in my life, probably a lot more than I let on to people, but I think it's all down to faith. If we know in our hearts that God is in the driving seat, in control, then as Lecrae would say, that is Real Power! Knowing this then, we behave in a way of contentment, and we do not let Fear take the steering wheel. When this happens, the worry and fear grow like cancer; out of control until it becomes a habit of our lives. When this happens, we should go back to scripture and remind ourselves that God is our strength and refuge and ever present help in times of troubles. If not, we are ruled by fear. He takes a seat at the top of the food chain and dictates our decisions and future where we do not see the fullness of God's promises. With the word of truth comes faith, and that is how I have decided to not try my hardest to live. From this, we talked about ways she could put a positive spin on the incomes that life had given her, so that they did not determine the life outcomes. I felt really urged to push her into something she didn't particularly want to do. I felt God just saying, "When you do this, I will heal your heart." God works in the most mysterious ways, but his ways are not our ways, and we should never forget the power of that. When we forget that power and remove him from our driving seat, we walk alone and decrease the room for the impossible to become possible. The bible doesn't say that we can do all things, it says we can do all things through Christ who strengthens us. How loving is our God? He tells us that all we need is Faith, and then provides us with the Faith we need!

Helplessness has to be one of the most unpleasant feelings ever, and is so counter productive in getting things done. It's also tough when trying to make room for God to work; knowing all you want to do is help, but by no means what-so-ever being able to, and putting trust in what we do not see to be in control of the situation, even though all we want to do is run with our kite. This is a summary of my feelings sometimes. This 'great wait' does get the better of me, and the feeling I dislike the most is helplessness. I feel a little like Rapunzel locked up in her tower, having something amazing to share with everyone but not able to do so.

This has often brought me to tears. Tears of confusion and hurt and frustration. Sometimes the feeling of, *Why do you not want me out there on the battlefield doing your good work?* would often come up in my conversations with God. I don't know why God wants me to be in the situation I am right now. I do know that I don't like it very much. I feel like I am swimming in the ocean with no land to be seen, but I do know that God doesn't put you somewhere that he does not want you to be. I have also realised that he will not put you somewhere that you aren't ready for. Furthermore, he will not put you somewhere that other people are not ready for you to be, and boy they were not ready for all this. This one particular instance, I was so mad at the deal I was being dealt. I couldn't take joy in my trials because I just wanted to be out there. The infantry of the army. Doing what I love and know. My impatience reminded me of a situation in the bible where Paul is denied entry to Asia twice. His account when he returns explains exactly why. He tells of how ghastly it had been and how they had nearly all died, and that was after God's preparation. Imagine if he had gone in his own time. He would have been over his head and possibly even died. It is nice to be reminded, when you can't take joy in your trial, that God has a master plan to go with his master key. And we are entitled to both, of which release Heaven here on earth. It is also comforting to know that God is preparing us for a time of breakthrough. It is also common to question God why this is happening, and to not even take into consideration that it's the Enemy's strategic plan to make us crumble. Satan and his cronies will try and destroy our relationships and all our motivation for the advancement of the kingdom. Even in times where we wonder and question God, he's telling us that he's right there with a plan already unfolding. He's holding our hands and squeezing them tight and reminding us that he has placed a divine calling on our lives. So when we face trials, or when we feel attacked by the Enemy, it is often because we are doing something right, opposed to something wrong. He fights against those worth destroying. He won't waste his time on people who aren't going to make a difference, start a revival, or change the world!

God isn't likely to hand it to you if you sit around waiting for it. You're never going to learn that people come before you if you're not out there working for them. What better way to become a servant than to serve? God's healing powers and directional openings quite usually appear when we lose ourselves and love other people. What better place to see God than in doing something for others whilst screaming out for help ourselves? Although, at these times, it is when we find it hardest to want to do anything, never mind help someone, it is also these times when we see our truly blessed lives from a different perspective; the 'it could be worse' perspective. This, in turn, can give us a drive to reach out our hands to those who need it.

When I was growing up, if we didn't do our homework, it wasn't likely that we would get to play out with our friends. I remember my brother really struggling with this. He is quite the opposite of me; incredibly dependent. Although with age this has dissolved a little, when we were younger, he couldn't do anything by himself, or for himself. Whereas I was opposite, I was incredibly independent and don't ever remember asking for help. God wants us to find a healthy medium. He needs to know that we need him. He also needs us to go out there and do what he's told us to do: help those less fortunate than ourselves. We should treat others as we would want to be treated. When we are feeling down, would we want people to not help us out? Give us an encouraging word? Spend time with us? Or just be there in general? I know I hate that! More than anything, all I want when I'm feeling down is to be surrounded by people. People who understand me. Who will help me in love. People who care for me.

Serving doesn't mean that you are below other people. It means you know you are seated high with Christ, who then shows you how to become less like you and more like him.

Grace > Helplessness

CHAPTER 9

If you want to walk on water you have to get out of the boat

I know, right now, where I would like to be and what I would like to do, but getting there has proved to be difficult. Doesn't it always seem that way? Taking that initial step of faith was holding me back. It's not, by any means, a lack of trust in God, because I know that he never leaves a good work unfinished. I have less and less doubt daily about his plan and more encouragement in the situation. It's man I have little faith in. It's man that I don't trust. This can prove to be very difficult seeing as it is man that we deal with daily. Nevertheless, I guess we have to see the potential in people that we would want them to see in us, and this is proving to be incredibly challenging. Where do you draw the line?

People generate the thought that they are this one tiny person operating in a huge world, and yes, this is true, but what you cannot underestimate is the impact you have on the world around you. That's where my doubt comes in. It is so massive as your decisions can have a domino effect and change the community you live in and the nation and even go on to changing the world. Sometimes, it doesn't always have to be positive change. It can be incredibly negative change; we see it around us daily. Moses was just one person and he led slaves to freedom! We are more than merely a shadow, but we serve a lord who is greater than any shadow we create or any issue we face. So then what are we actually capable of? We underestimate the work we do as impacting one person's life can affect multiple lives and one word can make or break someone's day. There is a nation inside of you.

Something that I have realised recently is that I guess it doesn't really matter what my plan is, because God will use it regardless to glorify the kingdom. He will bring good from any situation we face and he will grow and develop plans. There is always method behind his incredible madness and sometimes we're not always in a situation where we can have a physical tangible impact on someone's world. What I have realised is that God makes even small things impact and small things possible. It is the fact that we believe God will multiply our efforts or finances, or time, that we sow into his plan. Man will plan his steps but God will direct his path. You literally do not know the opportunities God is going to put in front of you. Since leaving the United States, I took it upon myself to carry on mentoring some of the people I had started to do so whilst out there. Via Facebook, this can be incredibly difficult when they're upset or angry or lonely, because all I want to do is hug them. Be that as it may, the almighty God has proved himself faithful to his promise and will also finish the good work he has started. It has also shown me just how powerful words can be. Words that we speak. Words that we write. Most of all, words that we think. Our thoughts determine our actions and that is incredibly powerful. Life and Death are in the tongue. That's such a powerful expression, such a powerful piece of scripture, but when you actually realise that God spoke the world into life, he spoke Adam into life, and he speaks us into life, you see that we have that same power. The power that rose Christ from the dead. The words we speak over people's lives are declaring something for them. The words we speak over our lives are declaring something for us. What is bound on earth is bound in heaven. Are you declaring the truth into someone's life, or are you declaring death over them?

We were given an authority and if we truly understood how powerful we actually are, we would be blown away. I often sit and listen to people who are so anointed and I say to God, "I want that. What they have God I want." And what he keeps reminding me is that I already have it. I just need to tap into it. I need to be sure that I find my identity in Christ, the creator, the biggest most powerful thing, and because of that, things are about to get crazy. It's not that I am not ready. It is that you're not ready for me. It's cool though; I will wait. God's timing is perfect.

It is quite funny that when we think we have no options, when we have no one to impact or nowhere to go, God often pulls something out of the bag. I have gone from having no options to multiple. God's big plan has gone from me 'knowing' where I want to be and finding myself somewhere completely different on so many occasions. If you look back, I am sure that you can see this happen in your life too. So this obviously has stressed me out. If you know anything about me, you will know I am the biggest control freak on the planet and I like to have a plan. I like to be in control and I like to know that if something goes wrong, I can solve it; or that I can fix it. But what I didn't realise until now is that I can't fix everything, and I also cannot be in control of things that are beyond my control. How can I try and take control of the almighty creator? What was really going through my head? Did I think that I could do it better than him? Because time and time again, he has proved that pointer incorrect. Who knows … but anyways, for the one hundreth time, I realised I am not in control. And although this scared me, I also felt a little free. Free to make mistakes. Free to make choices and not stick to plans. Free to do what I want to do and find myself in my way, the way God created me to be. My trust doesn't need to be in man, it needs to be in God. God knows that we are going to get lost.

He knows that we aren't going to get it right. But like a caring parent, he tells us where to meet him again and that's the cross.

All my life I have had a plan. I have had trust in myself and my own ability to be able to be, and do, what I want. Growing up, my dad always said two things to me: "Sam, the world is your oyster." and, "If it was easy, anyone could do it." Motivational right? I was adamant that I was going to go all the way through school and get my PHD. So adamant that this was my life plan. I was going to be so successful and this would be measured by my level of qualification and my salary. After my second trip to camp, this wasn't my plan anymore. God changed my heart so that I realised, *what does it matter if I have a library's worth of knowledge, if I don't know the love of God, and that he calls me to qualify me for what he needs me to do. Regardless of which, what use is that knowledge if I spend forever learning it and never putting it into practice? What use is it to me if I don't share it?* This realisation led to me pulling out of studying my masters, much to my Father's dismay. I no longer want to study my life away academically. Not even theologically, because the realisation that there is more to life meant more to me. It did, however, mean sacrificing my control over things. It also made me realise that I do not need trust in man. I don't even need trust in myself, I just need trust in God. So I walked into an Administration Job for a company I knew little to nothing about. A place I didn't ever see myself, but an opportunity God had blessed me with. Every opportunity is a blessing. Another chance to become more like Christ. Another chance to give God more of our trust. Another chance for him to prove himself faithful. The miracles and favour I have seen in my place of work are literally countless. I have seen promotion and responsibility that only could have come from God's blessing. I have made friends there that have hugely impacted my life to the point where they even think that God put us in each other's paths. How incredible is he? At this point, I was reminded of scripture, in Mark 4. So

Jesus and the disciples decided to go out in a boat. I love going out in boats, especially if the weather's nice, but it has to be nice. Otherwise, your hair gets wet and it's all stuck to your face. You are just absolutely freezing your socks off and those times are not nice to go out on the boat. Anyway, Jesus is out in their boat and it's night time, which I can't ever really say I have experienced. Do boats have headlights? Jesus is flat out on his pillow catching some Z's and a storm starts. This obviously scares the disciples to death. They start freaking out and decide that it's best to wake Jesus up. He always knows what to do and they were probably all close to vomiting or crying. I can imagine it was one of the worst feelings ever.

Jesus gets up out of bed, goes outside, and REBUKED the storm. So basically tells it to stop. And it does so like it was nothing! Now if I were there, I would have been bemused, amazed, shocked (probably in a worse state than I was when the storm actually started), but Jesus just strolls in like it's nothing, which to him it isn't. And he snaps at the disciples, "Are you kidding? You have me in your boat and you're scared of a little storm?" (That's paraphrased of course.) At this point, I would have probably felt super awkward; like, "Yeah, you're onto something there Saviour, but man, I was scared!"

How can we be scared when Jesus is in our boat? Do we not trust what he is capable of? He is in each and every single one of our boats, sat right next to us the whole of the journey. He even has a boat for himself, ahead, leading the way, and also behind, pulling up the ranks. He is for us. He strengthens us. And he loves us. So why, sometimes, do we put him in a box like the disciples did that night? Why do we contain his authority and power and decide that things will work out best if we are in control? Why do we doubt the trust we know we have in him? God cannot be contained. He cannot be lessened or belittled, or even restricted. He is greater than ANYTHING! Why would we ever want to be in control? So maybe sometimes, it is good to take a different route and have a change of plan. I don't know what goes through my head sometimes, but I do know that I am not the only one to try and contain God and presume that he isn't as great as he is. I also know that I am not the only one to proclaim, with my tongue, that I trust God, and yet when push comes to shove, don't believe until he shows me he is trustworthy.

God is the definition of trustworthy he is love.

Grace > Fear

CHAPTER 10

Have your cake and eat it too

It is in our human nature to want. To constantly want the next best thing. To want the ten second wonder in your life. To want that which you cannot have. To want what is not quite right or ready for you. I go through stages of life; one moment I am so content, and the next thing I know, I am shopping and wanting all these amazing things. My best friend, Hayleigh Maxfield, is a serial shopper, and when we are together, it is guaranteed that we are going to spend lots of money and time 'wanting'. It's not often that we spend time together, but when we do, we make sure we make the most of it. We shop until we drop, and we have an amazing time doing it. Hayleigh Maxfield is the definition of a diva. She is always looking incredible and she is always on top of trends. She always has the designer handbag that is in at the moment, or the new tattoo that has been perfectly inked on her. She sets a pretty high standard in our relationship and encouragement of love for beautiful things, of which I am thankful for. I don't actually know what I would do without her you know. She was my wing man for a very long time. We did everything together. Chased guys together. Partied together. Cried together. And in all honesty, she has always been there through thick and thin. I have some of the best memories with her. Some of the best times in my life. Some of the most amazing celebrations I have had, she has been there. She is one of those friends you just never lose and it doesn't matter how many miles apart we are, or how often we speak, our relationship is still as strong. I just want to take this time to honour her and to thank her for never leaving my side. When I realised that the things of the world didn't satisfy me anymore, she never discouraged or abandoned me, but showed me true love and compassion, and for that I am thankful. Here is to many more years to come making valuable memories …

Along the way, I have figured out that those things don't fill or satisfy me anymore, or if they do, it really isn't for all that long. I have also realised that what we should really yearn for is the love of God. For his will to be done here on earth as it is in Heaven. For those who don't know him to come to know him. And for peace to be upon us. This want turns to hope in the lord and being hopeful is commended! We should want God to plant the desires of his heart into our hearts and not be led by the desires of the World. Things do not make you happy. All you are doing is filling the yearning God put in your spirit and heart for him with other things.

Birthdays have always been my favourite celebration. There's something quite amazing about gaining another year of age, wisdom, lessons, etc. It is always nice to have everyone you love together to celebrate there with you that God has blessed you with Life. Beautiful right? My celebrations never last a day either. It is literally like a birthday week, and if I can get away with it, a birthday fortnight! This is also the perfect time to eat lots of birthday cake, which I absolutely love! My twenty-second birthday came in like a whirlwind; this happens most years with my birthday, being fourteen days after the New Year. Getting back into the habit of daily schedule can often steal time from us. This year, a dread crept upon me. This year, I was not looking forward to my birthday. As a matter of fact, I would have happily let it pass by like a summer breeze. The holidays had been my least favourite times, in my time being away from loved ones. It brings out a side of you that you only hope not to see. It can open a door to bitterness and resentment, and pull the rug from under your feet, leading you into a downward spiral of 'self pity' and condemnation. Being away from all those people, and at the time my better half, during times of celebration was always going to be difficult. By grace, God saved me from myself. I did want to have my cake and eat it too. I wanted every single one of my loved ones to be gathered together, near or far, but this was impossible. I knew this, so I had already checked out before my birthday had checked in. This is something God very clearly saw, and by his great love and mercy, had superior plans for my favourite celebration; the one I had convinced myself would be just another day. God used the people around me to show his great love for me and to remind me that he knows, more than anything, how I am feeling, and the yearning going on in my heart. God sent angels from all over the country to visit me on my birthday. I had visits from people I missed dearly. I was spoilt by those angels close by. I saw the miracle of snow which kissed everything it touched so delicately as a reminder that God's love never fails or gives up … ever. I spoke to people across the sea and I received wishes of blessings and happiness from every corner of the globe. I brought in my day of birth with the love of my life via skype. He was so close. I wish I could have touched him. Watching him wish birthday wishes was so valuable. Not having one thing bring me down and having God in control showed me life in a whole new colour. There was not one point where I did not feel blessed. Not one moment I wished for things to be different. It was perfect.

I spent the rest of the holidays wanting my cake and to eat it too. Nothing was good enough. The blessings I was seeing daily didn't quite cut my high expectation of our glorious God. I was selfishly waiting for a miracle. Waiting for the impossible.

Waiting for God to pick me up and place me in the heart of those I love. When really all I had to do was turn around and accept the ways he had already blessed me, and all the people he had picked uniquely to be a part of my life to show me his amazing love. I counted others' blessings throughout the Christmas period and damned my own. Happiness will never come to people who do not already appreciate what they have, and the blessings they see in abundance daily. Sometimes, it seems that the dark cloud we are trying to fight off is consuming us at a vast rate and we are all alone in the storm. But God does want to bless us. And he does want us to feel his joy and love and peace. God is our silver lining in the midst of the hurricane that sweeps through our lives. God is too perfect for us to not see beauty in his ways and life. I feel people spend their lives living in the realm of what could be next, what will make them happy. Is it following a sign or wonder? A new car? A promotion? Being brought back to basics in my 'great wait' made me realise more than ever that some people don't have their cake, never mind the ability to eat it. People don't have the privilege of seeing an iPhone 4 as old, or want for a new kindle HD. Yet these people are the most inspiring of all, because they see what it's all about. They see the blessings that, as a western society, we dispose of too easily. They are 'poor' by our standards, yet so full of hope, joy, peace, and love. They value things that we take for granted. Things so simple as family, food, and a warm home. They understand the promises of God more than I think we ever will.

This is something that comes up so much in my life right now; taking things for granted. My relationships. My situation. My weaknesses and strengths. We, too easily, forget that these open doors to our prying Enemy, because he will never go somewhere he is not invited. We as a society have let him creep in through every pore possible to align our thoughts with his wants and needs, when all we should be doing is aligning up with our great creator. Captain Kim asked us once, "What priceless treasure are you in danger of throwing out simply because of the way it is packaged? Could it be the treasure of seeing him? Sometimes, God wraps his glory in hard circumstances of ugly obstacles, or painful difficulties, and it just never occurs to us that within those life-shaking events is a fresh revelation of Him." Wow! Just wow! So much power in that one statement! We can be so commercialized. We expect things to look amazing. We want our blessing and our miracle to come in the form of a blue Tiffany box, or with the red bottom of some Louboutins. I know I do! But in reality, we are blessed in the messy times. It is in those dirty, grimy, up to your elbows in it times that you are blessed beyond belief. You can be too busy looking for a sparkle that you miss the true light. It doesn't matter how many times you read James 1, which pleads us to take great joy in our times of trial. There is nothing like a personal revelation; without which, I don't think we quite understand how to take joy in times of trial. Like for real, how can you be joyful in a time where there really should be no joy? How can you smile and act like everything is going to be ok when really, on the inside, it doesn't feel like that? We need to learn how we can go out and shine our light. Live and shine, and not live and reflect the circumstances we are in. To show the love of our sweet Jesus to those lost and caught up in the stormy weather of society and its child snatchers who steal our hope and faith in our sovereign Lord.

During my time withstanding the 'great wait', I have fought a losing battle with myself. A fight that I had lost before it had even started. This fight was between the guilt and selfishness I felt when missing those that I love who were miles away. I tortured myself for a while; disallowing myself to share this longing to those who were so happy to have me back on their land - back in their lives and back where they wanted me to be. This never changed the fact that I longed to be somewhere else. I wanted my cake and to eat it too, and the dreadful sting of wanting to be somewhere else, somewhere I thought that God wanted me to be, prickled like a nettle. Every time I spoke to someone back in the states, I would yearn and miss them that little bit more and hate the United Kingdom so much more. My Durability through this time has been on a roller coaster. Some days, I would find my time here so pointless and meaningless, whilst other days, I saw glimpses of Heaven's plan for me. This rollercoaster of durability continues to melt corners of my heart that I wasn't sure existed. It's made me ask questions that I didn't think I would ever ask. It has prepared my heart for bigger and better things in the promise that God brings. Although I don't understand Jesus' ways sometimes, I know and trust him, and will gladly follow no matter how much pain I endure.

This is something that had taken me a while to work on, and something I will have to work on for the rest of my life. We can be very selfish when we think we are being selfless. I found myself thinking one day, *If only we could pay Jesus back for what he did for us. How could we go about doing it?* The thought of giving him my life, doing what he did for me, cropped up, and God's Grace hit me like a tonne of bricks. We will never be able to pay Jesus back for the price he paid for us. There is nothing we can ever do to deserve the gift of salvation. We are given the option. We are given life. We choose how to live it, and even our best efforts don't stop this life from being sinful. However, God knows that no one is perfect. There was once someone who was sinless, blameless. Someone who was love, but we crucified him. We murdered the message of love. And in this great sadness, God, being as graceful as he is, used it to the glory of the Kingdom, and turned it into a victory. A gift of which we don't deserve, but Jesus does. This grace and love was made very apparent to me during my birthday celebrations. I, a sinning human being, do not deserve half of the blessings God gives me daily. Blessings

I take for granted. Blessings I don't appreciate half as much as I should. But because Jesus fills the gap, I receive them fully from my hope and love. God fully deposits his desires into my heart.

God wants us to have our cake and enjoy it.

Death is an intriguing aspect. When I think of Jesus dying, it was just truly sacrificial, and for such an amazing cause. This isn't always true for everyone else's lives. At every age, for every reason, people die, and it can be so confusing. Demike and I found ourselves in a situation where we found death of a child we had never met. My blood type is O-, so when it comes to babies, it doesn't cooperate very well. How do you deal with that? I guess for a long time I didn't. I presumed that God didn't think that it was the right time for us to be parents, and that was easier for me than anything else. I thought he had a different plan, but God is life not death. It wasn't until a long time after it had happened that I dealt with it, and realised that God allows things to happen because his ways are not our ways, and his thoughts out reach our intellectual ability. However, I was still so confused about why, if he is life, he would let this happen. I was so convinced that I wouldn't be able to have kids. It was easier for me to pretend that I didn't want them, because it meant less hurt. It made it incredibly difficult when it came to accepting Faith, because it was something that I didn't think I would be able to give Demike. That I, as his wife, wouldn't be able to give him what another woman had, even though God knew how much he wanted it, and secretly how much I wanted it. God knows the desires of my heart and he has shown me my family with Demichael. He has visibly shown me what our family will be made up of. He is forever faithful to his children. We shouldn't just form presumptions of Him within our time of hurt. Don't accept the lie that the devil has put over your life. Demike and I will have children. We will have a family and we will see life, even in the dry bones.

Presumption and expectation are two very crafty pixies in life. They often bring disappointment and hurt, and are often caused by 'norms' produced in society, which as nations, we regard to be truth. This could not be farther from truth. We have no right to expect anything, and we also have no right to expect it to a predetermined standard! What society suggests is right for us, or what we should put up with, is not necessarily within God's will of fulfilment for us, as his children. I demand this! I deserve that! I am entitled to so on and so forth ... I want my cake and to eat it too, because I am deserving of that. The only things we can be declaring in our lives is God's truth and life, but we don't know what we are ready for. I led my life with the attitude that I deserved so much, not just from a career, but from a partner or other people such as an employer or colleague, etc. in my life. Although I was never set on marriage, or a family, I didn't see myself lonely. However, I don't think I saw myself with one person for the rest of my life. Society had hypnotised me into convincing myself that I wanted a hassle free lifestyle, that I deserved a man who had bank accounts in every country to go with his pent houses, and that I also owned multiple houses, a yacht, and multiple other items. I believed I should be whisked away for luxury weekends and spoilt with things unnecessary, not just by a significant person, but by me, because this is what I 'deserved'. These presumptions led me far from God's grace and mercy, and also into a fantasy world where nothing would ever meet my high expectations. The person I had fallen in love with didn't whisk me away for luxury weekends, because that just was not financially possible. I'm sure he would have done it if he could, but what I'm saying is I didn't love him any less for not being able to do that. It doesn't mean that I should have felt unloved and that I shouldn't strive to prosper. It means that my motives shouldn't be because I desire something. It means that God wants to bless me with those things because I am undeserving, not give me those things because I have done something to deserve them. We can never do something to deserve that. There is no act that can amount to a blessing, but we are children of the most high and that means he wants to bless us. The relationships that I maintain in life are now led by love, which is something that has taken a long time to happen. There was a time where I only entered a relationship, of any kind, after assessing what I would get and what I would lose from the investment. The expectation and presumption haven't stopped their cunning works in my life, but merciful ways of Jesus help me to acknowledge the fact that the only hope we should have is in the Lord our father, and that when we set these hopes into earthly things without his go ahead, this will lead to hurt, a hurt that he tries to prevent. Help we can sometimes choose to ignore.

We can expect God to be faithful to the promises he makes us. We can have trust and hope in those things. We can also expect God to answer our prayers. It is the presumption of how he is going to do those things that is our pitfall in our cake proverb. We cannot pray and commit to an all knowing, all loving, all faithful, all blessing God, yet not trust his ability to work in our lives. If we choose to live as forgiving and as mercifully and sweet as Jesus, when these expectations are broken, we will see the positive and not the negative. Trust me, I know this is hard. Being in the 'great wait' has brought many expectations of God, but also relationships I have and the way people behave. I am the kind of person who struggles sometimes when people don't see things the way I do, and growing up, this brought a lot of hurt and frustration to my life. I am now thankful that people don't, because the only way we should want to see things is Jesus' way. We cannot, however, have the best of both worlds. We cannot put our hope and trust in the things of this world, because they will disappoint. And we cannot live by the standard set by society, because that is not what God has set out for us. Knowing that the only perfect person to walk the planet was the son of God brings a humbling sensation when the pixies of expectation and presumption wreak havoc in our lives. So pray that God blesses you with the ability to see the desires of his heart, and know, and EXPECT, him to show up in your life. Just don't bring presumption into it, because he is guaranteed to surprise you.

Grace > Sitting on the fence

CHAPTER 11

Allowing the Teacher to Teach

People come in and out of our lives all the time. Sometimes, it's something we aren't even conscious of. Maybe we lost contact with someone or someone just slowly became less of a priority. Other times, this exit can be drastic. It can be you giving someone the boot, or even the other way around. I don't know which one hurts more, the realisation that someone didn't put enough effort into a relationship, leading to its deterioration, or that you didn't put enough effort, leading to someone making a very apparent decision to get rid of you. However, both of these situations can be in regard to the other person and their lack of effort, and that's the real hurt. Sometimes, it hurts the most knowing that you have done all you are capable of doing and that it still just wasn't good enough for them. That they viewed you as useless to them, at some point or stage. Like you were of no benefit to them anymore. Something that has challenged me in the time I would call my great wait is; who decides how much effort we put in? Who says when we put too much or too little in? I began to question myself. Can you ever put too much effort into a situation? What about when you are constantly losing the battle? Jesus never gave up. He didn't turn around in the garden of Gethsemane and say, "Y'know dad, this is too hard. I've decided not to take on the sin of the world. Those people can fight for their own freedom." No, actually, Jesus fought for our freedom. Our freedom to stand for a cause and to live and to have free will. To choose to love and to care. Even while knowing that we may never even acknowledge him or our glorious father. Galatians 5:1 tells us that it is for freedom that Christ has set us free. He set us free from the chains of condemnation and not being able to stand for what we believe. Paul then tells us that we should stand firm because we are no longer slaves. It is this freedom realisation that helped me to see that Demichael was put in my life, by God, *as a blessing* to teach me and help me. We need to be people who make a conscious decision that throughout any relationship we will use it as an opportunity to grow and sow, and not an opportunity to reap and creep. We need to allow our hurting situations, in particular our hurting relationships, to show the world the evidence it requires of our need for Jesus.

God tells us that we must love one another *as he has loved us*. God doesn't ever fail in his relationships, because he loves us. He doesn't decide that one day he will only put in enough effort to just get by. God is never just enough. No-one wants just enough. Just enough love or money or food. God is *never* just enough! Because of this, we must choose in our freedom from Christ to be more than enough. We are commanded to love like God has loved us. The word tells us that we must work at all we do as if we were working for the lord. I need to open my eyes to things unseen. The realisation that this season with him was vital in my walk with Jesus taught me a lot about my perceptions, my options, my hopes, and my dreams; and also the condition of my heart that was once again alive and beating. It took me flying back to the UK multiple times, in multiple different gruesome situations, to realise that I based a lot of my love for Demike on saving him from his situation. Although I told him I could never be his saving grace, I think secretly, I wanted to rescue him. I am a 'Mrs fix it'. I like to bring restoration. However, I did realise, even more so, that he was not the only person that I felt like this about – it was just easier to cover it up with him. I realised that I see people as a task; to help them fix things, or to help them figure things out. This made me question a lot of relationships, friendships, and mentoring situations in my life, and what my actual motive was. Was it to love them and to draw alongside them and enjoy life with them, or was it to fix them? It took me a while to realise really how destructive this could be and I had to decide to stop. To put down what belonged to God and to leave it with him and say, "God, this belongs to you …." I also realised that I can't live my life in a hope of 'what if?'. Jesus set us free for *today*. Jesus has blessing in the here and now. He has miracles waiting for us in this 24 hours of life that we are facing, so to base my hope on 'what if?' would be unrealistic. It also made me realise that I had faith *for* things; opposed to faith *in* something. Life and faith are not for the 'what ifs' of tomorrow. The word tells us that tomorrow shall worry about itself. However, Jesus has to be the reason we find freedom. We cannot live via someone else's freedom, because then we live like a parasite, sucking the life out of someone else and never being satisfied. Jesus is the only person who can fill us and make us full and overflowing. He is the only one who can provide us with a freedom that liberates, because true love liberates. Wanting to change for someone else will leave you half full. It will also start a fire of resentment in your heart that will grow and grow and grow until one day, you are suddenly ablaze. It will also lead to a very impersonal relationship with the father when he has given us the freedom for so much more. Jesus came so that we could have life and live it to the fullest. Not so we could latch onto people like parasites and feed off what they have. I find that when we are trying to fix a situation, opposed to love a situation, the person becomes dependent on us and not on Jesus. So often, I have found myself in situations where I have to remind other people, and myself, that I cannot do life for them. They have to make decisions themselves and they can only ever depend on God's prompting and faith. Jesus is standing there screaming out, telling you he is going to lead you to greener pastures with a future and a hope.

God doesn't want us to drown, and when you live off someone else, that is what happens. You encourage the other person to also drown. And that is where, not only me and Demike, but other different relationships found ourselves; drowning each other. We were pulling each other under on our way to the top and neither of us realised that Jesus was stood there, telling us to stop. That he was enough and that he could fix it. That he *wanted* to fix it. In situations like this, someone needs to let go before you drag each other down, before you're both at the bottom thinking, *Wow, that was a big drop.* Luckily, when we hit rock bottom, we realise that God is our foundation and that he was there waiting. Not to say, "I told you so," but to lift us on his mighty right hand and say, "Look, this is the way." The situation we find our relationship in right now hurts me. I mean really hurts me. The worst thing about the end of a relationship is that I genuinely grieve that person's presence in my life. Because I am so used to sharing things with them and doing life alongside them that, for that to be completely removed, it is as if I have a void to fill. On the other hand, I feel a sense of Liberation, a sense of freedom, a realisation that I can chose to love because God loves me, and that this is what Jesus died for. However, I also realised that I am not super woman, no matter how much I like to think I am. I personally *cannot* save people. I can do nothing alone. But with Christ I can do anything. Scripture tells me I can even move mountains, but ultimately all I can be is a vessel for God to work through me. And whilst he is working through me, he will bless me. As the river of life runs over my roots, I absorb the goodness of God.

The battle has already been won, but that does not mean that here on earth things are peaceful between us and our Enemy.

He is out to steal, kill, and destroy, and he will take you captive wherever he sees fit. Yet when we realise that Jesus is our life jacket, our liberator, then we realise that we don't need to save the world. Jesus already has. Our job is to show the world, to be a light, to help people see the jacket we should be clinging so dearly to, because then they see that that is how we do not drown. God is faithful to his promises that he proves to us daily. He is faithful to making us better people, the best we can be, and he does this by loving us and teaching us how to love wholeheartedly. It is okay to be vulnerable and to hurt, especially when our father is a great healer. But he also reminds us that we are *free to live* for today and not for the shackles of yesterday, because we should be the change we want to see in the world. We should not live in the future of wanting to be somewhere, of wishing something else would happen, because God is willing and prepared to bless us here and now.

Now I am a person who gets attached considerably easy, and from past experience this is always something that has led to more hurt than anything else. I am such an investor. I will invest everything I have into a situation, or a relationship, and I am just totally not able to do half a job. If I do then boy do I feel the guilt of it! One day, I decided that I wasn't going to be that person anymore. I wasn't going to allow myself to become vulnerable, or even give all of myself to any kind of relationship. And this was all good and well, because it kind of fell in the time where I moved away from home and started university. At this time, I was in and out of church, trying to people please and not actually knowing myself, what I wanted, or where I wanted to go. Thus being vulnerable wasn't really an option. However, I had also found that when I decide things, God takes it the opposite way of how I could have ever expected. At university, I met someone who would see me more vulnerable than any other human ever has and that's the most difficult part of loving without limits. It was also someone who, although didn't and doesn't believe in the love of Christ, would be used drastically to allow the teacher to teach me. Like I suggested before, some people come into your life for a season. Some, you are lucky enough to have for a lifetime and will constantly teach you things, not only about yourself, but about life. Kelsey Marie Urey is that person for me. We have been through hell and high water and God has performed miracle after miracle. He has also taught me through my friendship with Kelsey that because he has loved me, I can love wholeheartedly and that there is nothing I wouldn't do for someone I love. I understand a lot of what I've written been in regard to Demike, because he is my first real encounter of romantic love. However, behind the scenes, I have been learning and building up my heart and capabilities through my friendship with Kelsey. She has taught me more about selflessness than I could have ever imagined. She taught me how to be patient, how to apologise, and how to forgive.

Kelsey Urey is a character like none before. I have never come across anyone like her in my whole life and actually doubt I will ever meet a person who is as caring, kind, encouraging, hilarious, and matter of factly as she is. There is *nothing* that can stop her when she has her mind set to something, and she would go to the end of the earth to make you happy, to lift your spirit, and to inspire you to become the best version of yourself. She is the least judgemental person I know and can take everyone as they are, and at their exact walk in life. She is an inspiration and I am proud to say that she is my best friend. We have also made so many, many memories all over the world. One year, we went to France skiing with our other friend Sammy, who is also another devoted, incredible, encouraging person whom I am honoured to call friend. It was the most surreal experience ever. We literally partied in a street full of snow, in snow boots and thermals with cauldrons of mulled wine dotted everywhere, and crazy French people dancing all over the place. We lived together for two years and, during this time, some of the most insane situations occurred. Ones that you probably couldn't make up. One morning, I woke up to find Kelsey asleep in a shopping trolley – Duvet and all! Although during these times I didn't always make the best choices, and I didn't necessarily love Jesus or other people, or even myself for that matter, I did make friendships in this time with people who have proven to me that they will love me no matter what. They are dependable, they are encouraging, and they want to love on me, even during all the chaos and hurt they were there to stand with me. I dedicate my life to loving them like they have loved me and allowing Jesus to use me in their situations. I am not the person I was when we first met, but I am so sure that I want to show them a level of commitment that they have shown me, because through them, especially Kelsey, they have taught me so much about Jesus and about love that it is the only way I could repay them.

That is Jesus. Even when I didn't know him, I look back and see the work he has done in and through my life. Even when I didn't know him.

Grace > Being Stubborn

CHAPTER 12

Equality with Quality

I have never really considered my right as a woman that was earned for me long before I was even a thought in my parent's head. It's embarrassing really, because people died for me as a woman in society. But I have a few feminist friends that challenge me on day to day occasions and I think I have figured out that it's rude to disregard our ancestors sufferings for our blessings. Especially the accounts we have in the bible, because they are *real people* who lived and suffered real life things. Things that we often look at and disregard, because we don't think that it's relevant to our time. However, let me tell you, they are so relevant! It may not be the same society or the same scientific factors, but it is the same dilemmas that we face today. We are facing issues with sexual immorality and idolism, and the things that are different don't change the truth and life that God speaks into the situation. That truth is eternal and it will be applicable for the rest of eternity. However, whilst figuring those things out and trying to get to know Christ more, as well as trying to understand the different lives of the biblical characters more, I kind of lost myself in the question 'who am i?'. Who am I aspiring to be? Where does God want me? And what does he want me to do? Often in arguments/discussions with other people, I would ask, "Who are you?" and, "Where do you want to be?" Not because I didn't know already, but because I was so confused about myself and I didn't know what to do about it. I needed some inspiration. Some encouragement. A little push into a thought process that would help me realise my identity and my lineage, and my place on this crazy earth. I didn't even know where to start in regard to looking. There are so many magnificent people, especially women in the bible, that I couldn't possibly be like one of them - Sarah, Mary, Ruth, Rahab. One of my favourites is Esther. I always think of Esther as being secretly sassy, and that is an attribute that I would want people to see her in me. She showed up in the King's quarters knowing fine well that that in itself was enough to get her a one way ticket out of the palace, but she did it anyways to stick up for those she loved, and for what she thought was right. She could have been murdered there and then. She had been through the craziest few years of her life. First, being adopted by a Jewish woman then pampered into a beautiful queen. It was one extreme to the other and it really gets me thinking, *God adopts us into his Royal family to be used in the redemption of souls. We were made for such a time as this.*

"14 For if you remain silent at this time, relief and deliverance for the Jews will arise from another place, but you and your father's family will perish. And who knows but that you have come to your royal position for such a time as this?" (Esther 4:14 NIV)

This is inspiring, encouraging, and frightening all at the same time. Firstly, we are adopted into a Royal family – how amazing! But it doesn't stop there; we are to be used. We are significant and it may well be that we were called to be in our situation for a reason. Women were created to be at the right hand of man as a joint heir of our heavenly throne. So why is it that, even after so many women have died for equality, there are people still all over the world being exploited, used, sold, abused, and disregarded? According to the U.S. State Department, six hundred thousand to eight hundred thousand people are trafficked across international borders every year. More than seventy percent are female and half are children, and that is America alone. Women were not created to be the foot stool for man, or even to be regarded any lower than man. They were created to be equal, the other part of the deal, the ying to his yang, and so on and so forth. We were taken from Adam himself to walk by man's side.

The exploitation of women has forever been around and people have risen up over the centuries to give women a voice, a place on the throne, a right. And this is all good and well in society today, but what about those who have lost their voice? One of the most famous people to ever grace the planet, no not Jesus, but he regarded Jesus as the most greatest being to walk the planet, Sir Martin Luther King refused to accept black people as an inferior race. God had told us to love thy neighbour and that is what he preached. He didn't stop until something was done, until the eyes of this slumbering world opened. Why should women be seen as an inferior sex? Why should we be discriminated against because of our gender? Gender is a partnership where two very different creations should work together in harmony to glorify a great and mighty God. It is about time someone took a stand for those suffering, being abused, trafficked, and raped. Who gave men the right to preside over women? Who gave men the right to treat women as belongings? This is something I hear and see daily in the media, in music, on the television, and internet. Something I've even found myself involved in. You may question why this chapter is even all that relevant to my story and why I would ever include it, but I have experienced first hand the fact that women have been turned into lustful objects that should be used and abused to satisfy a man's needs, as if they preside over women. I had developed over the years a mentality that the attention I received from a male not only defined me, but gave me confidence to be who I thought I was. I allowed guys to use me for what they needed, thinking that it was that that I needed as well. I was manipulated emotionally to do things I probably didn't want to do all that much – do not get me wrong, a lot of the time, it was my decision, but that is where I had gotten so confused. I thought that it was in a sexual lustful encounter with a guy that i would find my identity, that it was who I was. I was designed and created to gratify them and that I also deserved gratification too. I couldn't even count on one hand how many times I have woken up in a strange place with a strange guy. And after that, I couldn't count on the other hand the amount of times I woke up with a stranger in my own bed. For the longest time, I enjoyed it. I found something in it that 'inspired' me. That that one night of excitement would be enough to push me through to the next eventful situation. I craved the attention of guys to the point where I look back and don't see a time where I didn't seek it, where I didn't go out of my way to do something to attract them to me, or say something to encourage their attention. I knew so very well how to play the game and I was very much a part of it, but it is because of times like these that people then believe that once you have changed they are still able to manipulate and take advantage of the fact that you craved that type of attention in your life. There was a time after I decided to live for Jesus that I found myself in an incredibly sticky and damaging situation, and yes, it did change me. Someone that I trusted, that had been there for an incredibly large part of my life, that had held me whilst I cried and encouraged me when I was down. They thought that they were able to take it upon themselves to behave a particular way with me, that they were able to intimidate me and take advantage of me. In this situation, I learned a lot of things. Primarily that we don't always know people as well as we thought we did, but also things such as sexual abuse and rape can happen to anyone, in any given situation, and it can be the least likely of people who will destroy the trust you had with them and abuse you, and your situation. Who gave them this right? That is beyond me and certainly from self. I am assured of one thing; there is one ruler in this Life, one person we should live to please, one person's love we should worry about. A merciful, graceful, loving ruler who would not dream of hurting, using, or disregarding us with disgrace and dissatisfaction. It is the prince of this world who does just that and encourages those blinded by his lies and schemes to also do so. God created women to be equal, so why is it not this way? I also learned that, in situations like that, we are not defined by how dirty and disgusting we feel. We are not bound by the unworthiness that creeps in. It is not our faults that we have been in that situation. It is *always* the person that has come against us. I spent a long time thinking that I deserved what had happened, because previously, I had been forward and allowed men to treat me like an object. However, even if I was still that person, it is not ok to take a situation into your own hands and decide that you have an authority in their life, and to take what you want from them. I am a new creation in Christ and that means I am protected. I am lifted up and I am worthy. I am respected and honoured and blessed, and those people who decide to ignore and miss this need prayer, and need it more than we will ever realise.

What will it take for people to realise that your surroundings do not define you? When you allow Christ in your heart, you are no longer able to be a product of your environment. You don't have to be what society tells you to be. This is not just for all you women out there, but also you men. You are called to be a chosen person. Someone who lives out their lives so differently that people question WHY. There is a live fire burning inside you. Burning for love, freedom, and equality to break free from the shackles of this world. Life's incomes do not determine life's outcomes. What will it take for people to wake up and realise this? There is not much point sitting around and waiting for a better day to come. This is something I learned hard and fast. That better day is today. Today is always the first day of the rest of your life. However, for as long as people 'love things' and 'use people', it is going to be an onward struggle and an uphill climb. It may feel like a losing battle, because those who are the hardest to love need it the most. But I have found those who need to escape the most have a list as long as their arm, full of ways the Enemy has convinced them they cannot overcome their situation, that God is not bigger than the problem they are facing. People need to realise, I mean really realise, that God doesn't make pie crust promises like us humans. The promises he makes in our love letter are real and he is faithful to those promises. He promises us a future and all we have to do is dream. Dream for the coming of the kingdom and we can't go wrong. Trusting in God is key to taking those first steps into the unknown. Into a place where you can't see in front of you. Into a Faith led, God centred life. For as long as you let your environment and upbringing apply boundaries to your life, you're not going anywhere. You're not getting out of that awful situation. Not experiencing that big wide world that we don't appreciate nearly half as much. This comes from knowing who you are and knowing your identity. So many people live under false names and false identities that they can never live life out to the fullest, because they don't actually know who they are. You are adopted. You are loved and you are in Christ! I'm not saying that it is that simple for everyone to just wake up one morning, pick up sticks, and move to a better life. But with God, all things are possible! Nothing good comes easily, rather it takes the realisation that, with God, you can dream and you can see your dream unravel into truth. Why don't you work towards that something today? Who knows, those first steps you make could help you figure out who you are. It is important that we remember to tell our problems how big our God is, not our God how big our problems are.

Grace > Inequality

CHAPTER 13

Grace

G rowing up in the world and having my heart transplant with my saviour so late in life has led me to some great difficulty with the term 'grace'. It isn't just myself that I know finds difficulty; I often see it in people who are my age and working on their relationship with God, and in a lot of the teens that I work with. It's the understanding that God, the creator, would do anything for us, because he loves us and not because of what we do. I came to the conclusion that the world, even some Christians, have this term all mixed up and wrong, and that we actually have no clue about real grace. It is so difficult for us to comprehend that someone would love and do things for us no matter what we have to offer. Living in a society where it is basic living to understand the phrase 'you scratch my back, I'll scratch yours' makes it so incredibly difficult to wrap our heads around the concept of grace, but we must understand it because we are called to show it. It is pivotal to understanding what God has done for us.

Grace is the most significant gift God has ever given us. We did not need to do anything for it, as applies with all of his gifts. It came through the death of his son, as a promise fulfilled from the old testament. It covers everything that we might ever do, say, want, or need. And we didn't have to do anything for it. It does not, however, excuse our sinful behaviour, because we know better. Not only do we know better, we are called to better. Every person on this planet will be, more often than not, put in a position where they have two choices: the easy option or the right option. It is hard to know which is which. And even if it is apparent, it is still challenging and we don't always pick the right one. However, grace is our band-aid when we trip and fall. It is our comfort and our refuge. Grace brought us our salvation. It is our ticket to eternity with Jesus Christ. It is more than enough. It covers a multitude of things. Nevertheless, we simply cannot get our heads around it enough to accept it. Grace is made most apparent when we are at our weakest. It magnifies God's power. It leads us and helps us through trials. And it keeps us from temptation. Yet we still struggle to understand it … more importantly we struggle to perform it.

As a follower of Christ, the scriptures imply that we need to apply grace within our own lives. Hebrews 12 talks about all the ways we must behave, and by doing so show grace. But even still, we simply cannot get our heads around it. Society, yet again, has set a standard, a boundary, on the way we not only behave, but what we stand for. This boundary has such a significant effect on our relationships and the way we treat people. But we merely forget that God is bigger than that. Grace is not an excuse for our behaviour, but an excuse to Behave! Grace is enough! God Declares in Corinthians 12:7-9 that his grace is sufficient. So why am I still struggling with it?

We forget to realise that grace can transform hearts. It can change the sinner to righteousness, because it brings out the Jesus in us. It helps us to not conform to the ways of the world, but to break those boundaries set by society, to serve a living breathing God. It reminds us that we are not of this world, that we are not called to live like everyone else. We are to be different, to be an anomaly. Grace reminds us of what we have to be thankful for, which in turn, leads us to serving. Serving not only God, but others as well. Our role is to soak up that truth. To breathe out the life of Jesus in our every breath. Ane to also be susceptible to change, because it is by God's grace and love that he turns us away from our past mistakes and makes us new in Jesus. Grace is such a radical idea; to love for no reason. To forgive for no reason. To turn the other cheek for no reason. Just grace. This is a selah moment!

Mid-journey, she informed me that they were talking about social support and how it is needed to overcome those things that life throws at us. Also, how it's important to draw together. She said that a really good example of this would be religious people. She said that the lecturer had said that when something happens, they draw together as a community and help build up that person again, back to their normal strength. How amazing is that? That it is a societal perspective that, as Christians, we are known to come together! This was positive and really made me feel warm and fuzzy inside. She went on to say that, socially, Christians support, not just each other, but the outer community, which we all already know another great positive example to the life of the church. But then she really dropped a bombshell … She said that her lecturer said that this wasn't always a positive, because yeah, Christians may go out and support the local community, but they often find that when the person they are helping informs them he does not want to be a part of what they believe, it is common for a Christian to drop away and withdraw support, and that this can socially make things worse. *Wow*! Right!

As soon as I heard this, I felt sick. So many arguments had started to draw themselves up in my head. I was actually enraged at that perspective. I mean that has to be the minority, right? It has to be the minority of Christians who behave that way, right? Instead of blurting all these things out, I bit my tongue for once and simply replied, "Oh, right. That's a sad perspective. Where do

I tie into it?" She then told me how she shared her story from the previous Sunday, where I had taken her to church for the very first time, and how at the end, when we were leaving, a couple came up to us and started asking us questions. She said that although she had told them she wasn't a Christian, this didn't put them off and they were still as interested by her, and in what she had to say as they were in me, who was a Christian. This was such an encouragement! We had not spoken much about her experience of church, although she had made it apparent she didn't agree with the idea of tithing, which was the preach that day, but that was about it. This was so overwhelming for me. I didn't quite know how to react. I sat there for a while silent as it sunk in, that she had witnessed grace first hand. Not just the grace of that couple, the grace of God. Although she hasn't given her life to Christ, she still attends church with me and she is still part of our small group … Do you know what you call that? Grace!

Breaking the silence like a popped balloon, she then told me that she spoke about how her best friend is a Christian (me), and how I never give up, regardless of a person's situation. And how I never stopped being a friend, even though I didn't always agree with the things she did even and had decided to pursue my relationship with God and leave the plans we had made as friends behind. This is *God's grace* first hand in my life. It is in situations like these where I miss that little factor and focus on things less important. When really, in this situation, all I had to be thankful for was God's magnificent gift of grace, but that wasn't always how I had felt when I encountered other Christians. It had been incredibly difficult and I often felt judged, so I totally knew where these people were coming from. I really struggled when I initially decided to be a Christian that I walked away. I turned my back on Jesus, because his people, that I had encountered, put forward a false pretence that they actually cared. Sadly, even now, I come across Christians who are so trained to pretend that they are interested and trained to be 'pastoral', but it is never about that. First encounter or initially being there. It is always about the follow up. It is always about the commitment. It is always about making a decision to think about that person often, and to check up more than that. This is why we are called to discipleship, to do life with one another.

We are to see that no one misses out on God's grace. Hebrews 12:15. Doing this can be so simple. Simple enough that we have not even realised we have been doing it already. Things such as the way we behave with strangers whom we briefly encounter in our daily lives. After returning from America, I had developed the habit of telling everyone I came into contact with to have a nice day. Honestly, I have no clue where I picked this up, but along with many other habits I did, that is so stereotypically American. Now every time I did this, I received looks of confusion. Not only from the person I was saying it to, but from the people I was with. My dad would practically rebuke the 'American' in me there and then. And the person on the receiving end would not have a single clue how to respond. They often just replied, "You too." But that tiny little sentence can make such the difference, and here it is breaking the boundaries of our society. So I am not going to stop.

Showing friends grace whom don't know the Lord can be difficult. I know this first hand. Not just grace for them, but showing grace for other people in front of them. One of my best friends, Holli Ann Davey, will tell you of this first hand. Not only that she thinks I am a fruit loop, but that she has just learned to expect the unexpected with me; which I can imagine can be difficult for her, knowing who I used to be. I cannot even begin to imagine, actually, how difficult it must be for someone you love and appreciate to so radically change, and you go on to carry on loving them, finding new ground to be common in, and things to appreciate together.

Praise the Lord for his grace and love! He had used me in that situation to show her that just because the rest of the world does something, it does not mean we conform. Sometimes, like I have said before, those that need love the most are often the hardest to love. And now, on a regular occasion, she will bring people to my attention who need prayer and who she thinks it may benefit for me to pray for. Grace is a term which has often been used to describe the more elegant, precious things in life. Things that may seem easier to break or destroy. But grace is not 'wimpy'. It is something that has more power behind it than we can imagine. It takes a lot of courage to act out in grace. When I was about seventeen years old, things got real tough in my family situation. There was a lot going on with my parents and I felt like I had no family to turn to. No one to lean on. No one to run to. My mum was hurting and my dad was off doing what he needed to do. I remember wishing that my family were as close as they had once been. Instead of being there, we grew apart. There were a lot of arguments over things that brought pain, and the situation turned very toxic. I stopped speaking to my aunts and grandparents and I stopped speaking to a lot of my cousins. Although my dad had defended me, we had turned our back on our family, because it felt like they had turned their backs on us. I am so thankful that God is a God of restoration. I thought that the rowing and ignoring and bitterness that was going on in my family would go on forever. However, what the devil intends for evil, God will always intend for good. And today, we come together as a family that love and care for each other, and puts the past behind them.

The fact that Jesus is found within us changes things a lot. It means that we have no reason to excuse our behaviour, because we should not be behaving in that manner. If grace is living inside us, if love is living inside us, if mercy, forgiveness, joy, patience, peace, kindness, gentleness, goodness, and self-control are all living inside us, then what excuse do we really have? And why are we not thankful that we have a heart inside us that beats right? Why can we sometimes forget to be thankful for the grace that God shows us?

Grace > Law

CHAPTER 14

Mrs Fix It

You can walk alongside others and encourage them to move forward, but inevitably, the final choice is theirs, and that is all we can do. Just like the saying, 'You can lead a horse to water ...'. This realisation has been difficult for me. Realising that I can't change things, that I can't Fix things. This, in itself, drives me crazy! I just want to fix things and make it right. I will never turn my back on people, and I find it so difficult in making decisions, especially in regard to the people that I love. I just want to make things right for them. I just want to help them do and be better. People cannot be led by people who are not ready to lead. And sitting around waiting can crumple your spirit, and can put out your flame. Furthermore, it can dampen your hope. We have to lead by example. I know I am willing to fight for what I have. I am willing to fight for those around me. I am willing to fight for your soul. So leading by example is all I have. Showing people Jesus by my actions is all I am about. I am not one hundred percent on what the future holds for me, or the other people in my life. When God is at the wheels of our lives, that's what is best, and his plans are right for us. Sometimes, people are at different stages in their lives. Some are ready to fly, while some are still gaining confidence. As long as we remember that just because we're in flight mode, doesn't mean that we cannot force or leave behind those who are not. The past few weeks have been increasingly difficult for me. I have realised things about myself that I never even knew. Such as; I can be incredibly insecure. I've always let my confidence rule out in me, and I think this has been a protection mechanism. Like a clock has a glass face and a book a cover. What I realised is that you don't have to let that go, you don't have to be completely vulnerable. God knows. God uses those things to make you the person you are. But he also tells us to guard our hearts, not from him, but in regard to other people. Those protection mechanisms are there for a precise reason, and it is life experience that will highlight them and it's Jesus that will heal them. In this great wait, I have been freaking out over the smaller things. Having too much time on your hands isn't healthy. God tells us, in Genesis, that he created Adam to work the land. Our minds were created to be active, healthily active. On multiple occasions, a doubt that I didn't think I would feel again has entered my thoughts. Worry has plagued me, but at the end of it all, God has pulled me through, reminding me that he is my strength and refuge, and ever present help in times of troubles. And also that I can help myself. I can get over this analytical, tangible time I'm living in, and put my faith in the unknown. This, for me, has been very difficult. For the past five years, I've been training and developing my analytical, critical skills and it is very hard to not let them override the love in my heart that should conquer all.

Today, I found myself in two places; James 1: 5-8 and Proverbs 28:1. Both talk about divides within our personality, and God has made me consciously aware that when things go wrong, I jump off the wagon into the mud and give up all hope that I had accumulated. And for what? To start again from the beginning, when we serve God we need to have faith in him and only him. In what he is able to do. In what he has promised to do. In what he WANTS to do for us. Nothing else has the ability to satisfy our hunger, and sipping from two different drinks can be a lethal mix. This journey I am on is one that has forced me to constantly battle with my faith and my fear. And as consuming as fear can be, Faith wins everytime! God strengthens me and encourages me and loves on me, particularly in the times when i feel so far away from him and his plan. As well as the times where I don't feel like reading my bible, and the times I feel too exhausted to go to church. *He is with me!* However, allowing our mind to take control of everything can encourage us to have our cake and eat it too. And with God, that's not the case. You cannot have the best of both worlds. You have to make a conscious decision of who your God is and what he means to you. A great analogy that my friend Amy would use is, "Which wolf are you feeding? The wolf of fear or the wolf of faith?" This really just spoke to me, in regard to the future of other people. I can only have faith for them. I cannot fear the choices that they will make – that is not my burden and not my responsibility. This has been an incredibly difficult pastoral lesson to learn, but it often comes from insecurities, and a fear of feeling hurt. Of being disappointed by people or discouraged by them. But that will happen. We have a circle of control and that is our self, our reactions, and our feelings, which does not include or involve anyone else. *So guard your hearts*, because you cannot fix everything. Only Jesus can do that.

Grace > Being in Control

CHAPTER 15

ME

All my life, I've wanted to be good at something … dancing … swimming … education … sports … you name it, I probably tried it. I was on the Hockey team for a short while, I played Netball, and I did after school Dance and Drama; I tap danced. I would try so hard, but it never quite happened. Thus I would quit before I failed, because I was too scared of failure to carry on. As I got older, I wanted to be the hot attractive person who all the boys liked and got all the attention. And who was always in the boys' 'Top five' (this was a list every teenager had of the top five boys that they had a crush on), and always had some boy on her arm. Again, that didn't quite happen the way I'd have liked. I wanted to excel in something, to be recognised for being good at that something. Just any kind of recognition for being better than the next person, for being admired or acknowledged or just noticed. It wasn't until I reached twenty two that I realised what I'm good at. *I'm good at being me!* And 'me' is good enough. Yeah, sometimes I might be the me that screws up and hurts people, makes bad choices, and does stupid things … but I'm also the me that *loves me with all of my heart* and cares more than people think I should. Me is good enough: good enough, because I have been set free … by someone who made me … to *excel at being me.*

However, something that I have realised the more and more life experience I have is that the me growing up set some pretty stubborn coping mechanisms and barriers up to prevent myself from being hurt. More often than not, subconsciously, I need that recognition to let me know that I am doing a good job, and this massively affected my prayer life more than anything. I really struggled to pray and not get an immediate verbal answer. I also really struggled with just being able to pray an average prayer. I felt I had to make every single prayer so full of scripture and articulate it perfectly. And if I am being honest, it is still something that I battle with and it is a massive struggle to journal my prayers and just write down little small prayers. It had a massive impact when I found myself in times of desperation and all I could really do was just cry out the name of Jesus – in those times, I had nothing more to offer. But it is in those times that I feel God showed up in front of me with recognition.

This really set me off thinking, *I am so hard on myself about my prayer life all the time – I should pray more. I should pray for more people. I should pray for more things.* You constantly have it drilled into you that, "Prayer is powerful!," or, "Pray continually!," and, "Have you prayed?,"or even, "I will pray for you." All these things got me so bogged down, to the point where it became obedience opposed to an overflow of my heart. The prayers I would say were so far from sincere and more a duty. And, to an extent, I believe that this is ok when we have to remind ourselves. But I got so consumed by making sure I did it, opposed to actually caring about the thing I was praying about, and that showed in the times when I feel like God answered my prayer and the times I feel like I probably forgot what I was even praying about. When it is a cry from our hearts opposed to a formality of being a Christian, it becomes so much more powerful. So then it doesn't matter what you say and how you say it, it's about where it is coming from.

Prayer – "an earnest hope or wish, a solemn request for help or expression of thanks addressed to God."

As I just continue to go through everyday life, I realise and learn more and more about the nature of Jesus, and how my wants and needs are not always beneficial for me. And how God knows exactly what is right. I constantly live thinking that if I know everything about someone or a situation, that I am in control and that I know exactly what's going on. In some strange way, it makes me feel like I have a stronger connection with that person, meaning I love them more, and for them to tell me they love me more. And yes, I can understand why this may be; people don't reveal things to people unless they feel secure and safe, and this often comes with love. However, in reality, learning everything about everyone and everything removes the mystery of life. It removes the fire and passion you generate for someone or something. Jesus goes through life giving us snippets at a time about himself and his majestic ways. If he revealed it all to us, not only would we be bemused, but we would lose our zeal to find more to learn more, and to want more of him. I think this applies to our earthly relationships too. If we know everything about someone, we lose our fire to learn more, to grow more, and to enjoy things more. I am constantly hungry for something. I rarely feel satisfied for very long. I am just the kind of person who wants to be doing something more, finding God in a new way, and just moving forwards. And I just constantly find myself in a time of wait. If I have learned anything in my whole twenty three years of life, it is to 'Just let God'. Let him direct your path. Let him direct your prayer. Let him direct your passion as he gradually reveals himself and his glory to you.

Learning is a blessing that we often overlook. I love learning. I think there is something so unique about learning something new about something or someone. When you learn something about someone, it's like a new door has been opened and you see things so differently. It's just the same with learning about Jesus and his ways. He often takes us away to reveal himself like he did with Peter, John, and James. God set a precedent of leading people to a mountain to reveal him to us. This is true to our lives as well – he will bring us to a trial to reveal his majesty and his glory. He will allow us to enter a situation where only God can show up, or where we have to become dependent on him. I think he also does this, so that we do not grow comfortable. Being comfortable is so dangerous. We often meet God on the outside of our comfort zone, doing things that we don't always feel comfortable doing. I want to constantly view God in a different way. To constantly have my views and beliefs and perspectives shattered. For God to reveal himself in ways that keep me wanting more and intrigued about who he is and what he is showing himself to be. However, something I think I sometimes get trapped in is the difference between learning about God and getting to know God. It is so important to learn scripture, because it reveals God's nature to us. But I have found it even more important to have personal revelation about that scripture. I found myself in a position where I knew lots of scripture and I could probably recite it, but I didn't actually know God for myself. I hadn't worked on my relationship with him. I had been neglecting him, and I had a firm realisation that our relationship with God is just like any other relationship. In fact, it is a reflection of our relationship with other people. It needs to be invested in and it needs attention and time and love. Lord, we should enjoy your mystery and keep wanting more of you, and wanting to know you more. No one is perfect and we are designed to be us, specifically as God designed us to be.

Grace > Who we think we should be

CHAPTER 16

You best believe this is a war ...

What I want you to know is that God has an assignment for you. It doesn't matter who you are, what you are doing with your life, what you have planned, how qualified you are, what your skills are, what you like and don't like, or even if you want to do it or not, there is a calling placed upon your life from before you were even thought to existence that is *significant*.

After I first gave my life to Christ, I remember every night for the first few months I would have nightmares. I would wake up each and every single night tormented, worried, scared, sweating, and even panicked about what had happened in my dream, what had been tormenting me. Some nights, I would wake up because I could literally feel like something was standing so close to my face that it would startle me.

Other nights, I would wake up with what felt like hands on my back, and they would leave a burning sensation that would last for the rest of the night, almost as if some red hot hands were burning my back. Can you imagine what this was like? I was petrified! I remember at one point thinking I had literally lost the plot, like I was not sane and it was all some big cult and someone had put a spell on me.

From the day I gave my life I was attacked spiritually. Those four months, I literally don't remember much more that could have happened. I was taunted, I was stalked, I was intimidated, and I was manipulated. One night, I was in bed speaking to my friend on the phone and I heard someone outside my house. It sounded like they were trying to get in the back door. Obviously, I was a little freaked out – at this point my dad had moved out of the house so I had stepped up into the protector role and I felt like I had a lot of responsibility. The noise stopped and I had managed to convince myself that I was just going a bit mental again. Then I received a text message from a number I don't know, and at this point, stuff got real. Someone texted me saying, "It's ok, I know you are in the house, don't be scared." At this point, I am thinking, *what?* So I text the number back, asking who it was, and to this day I never received a response. I was really freaking out! I could literally hear my heartbeat in my ears. Then I heard someone come into my house through our back door. It sounded as though they had unlocked the door with some struggle and they were in my house. Now, as things were still crazy within my family situation, my mum was sleeping downstairs, and as much as I was in the role of the protector, I was scared. In fact, I was literally petrified and, looking back, if I am being totally honest, I do not have a clue why. I am not scared of anything like that. I am logical, and typically I would think of steps on how to resolve the situation. But I was certain that my mum would just wake up and deal with the intruder. However, she didn't even murmur. There was not one sound from her, not even a twitch. The next thing I know, I am so consumed by fear that I literally feel like something is on top of me, pressing me into the bed. I literally CANNOT move. All it feels like I can do is move my eyeballs, and that wasn't going to stop this intruder. I know sometimes this happens when we are so consumed by fear that we convince ourselves we cannot move, like a sheep in headlights, but I am telling you, there was something spiritual going on. I managed to will myself to grab my phone and call my dad and get him to come to the house, because I was so certain that there was someone in the house. Like, I cannot even explain how certain I was. That was the longest twenty minutes of my life. As soon as I had put the phone down I was so afraid. It was a fear I can't even explain.

At this point, I had only known of Jesus for a few months. The thought of any kind of Devil trying to scare me into the wrong direction was insane, I was very aware of the Devil. One of my God mum's favourite lines was, 'Do you believe in the Devil? Because he believes in you'. So I was aware; but I had no maturity, I had no wisdom, I had no memorised bible verses or even biblical knowledge to realise that no weapon formed against me will prosper. I literally had no clue about the spiritual realm, about the heavens and the earth, and this world that we live in. I had no idea of generational curses or things that could attack us, or spirits of evil, about angels or their armies; I had *no clue*. So I allowed the devil to taunt me, to victimise me, to pervert me, to use me. It wasn't until I had literally reached tipping point that I allowed him to get what he wanted, It reached the point where I had given up. It was more convenient for me to not be a Christian because I couldn't deal with all the psycho crazy things going on than it was to actually follow and believe something I didn't even know that much about. As much as I was convicted, it wasn't enough for me to stay. My tipping point I remember vividly; was when I literally allowed my friend to be in a situation where she was raped by a guy no one could ever find, no one knew or had seen, or could even be found on CCTV. Strange, right? This literally pushed me to walk away from God and the fullness he had to offer. But you better believe that I am not the only person that this has happened to. I am certain the Enemy has gotten people to walk away for less. There is a dirty, big fat word that I can think causes most people to leave … Offence. When people come to know Jesus they are walking in their calling, they have taken the first steps to their God-given dream, they have stepped into the potential that God has given them, and they are going to make a difference. It is their authoritative position here in this world to go into the whole of it and preach. To publically proclaim and to earnestly advocate *the truth*.

You think the devil isn't going to try and come against that? You think that when we're leading people to salvation, we should not wise up? We should not teach our brothers and sisters the reality of it? *We are at war!* However, just because we have victory, doesn't mean that the Enemy will stop attacking us. And he didn't. I literally remember telling someone in my church how I felt and that was it for me. I moved back to Uni. and back into the old lifestyle, and all that it had to offer. As much as God is able to do anything, the Holy Spirit is a gentleman, and he will not push his ways into a situation. And he sat and he waited, but boy was he powerful. When I look back at all the crazy that happened that year, I had the protection of heaven's armies over me more than ever before.

Just because Jesus has the keys, that does not mean that the Enemy isn't going to try and sabotage everything He has planned for us. He has come too far now to turn around, to give up, and to walk away from something he has started. I walked away from Jesus, because the hope that the church told me he offered wasn't the hope I needed at three o'clock in the morning when I felt like I was being attacked with fiery hands, or when I had dreams that I was underneath the spirits of the other realms. What I needed was the realisation of *who I am in Christ*, of the authority I have over all the Earth, over all the heavens, the same authority that Jesus was given – *He gave to us*. We totally live in sheer ignorance of this gift, me included. Instead, we pray for an easy life. We pray, 'Oh Jesus, please provide this, oh Lord God, please heal this. Oh

Jesus, please stop this.' Wake up and realise O'sleeper, you have the authority of heavens and earth. You are the body, Jesus is the head, and everything else comes underneath your foot.

Now, I understand that not every Christian who is saved will have crazy spiritual experiences. And I used to wish that I could say that those were the only crazy spiritual experiences I have had, but that's not true. There have been many, many, many situations where I have experienced the spiritual realm for myself, and yeah, it scares me, and yeah, I sometimes think, Oh my goodness this is not happening, and yeah, sometimes I feel like I am so fearful, but I am blessed with the ability to see what other people don't always see. For the longest time, I would think that I was going crazy. I understand that God gives us a vision of how he has planned things and I see that. One time, I saw my whole campground within one building. This building was basically more like a garage and it had around ten garage type doors that closed around it, it was huge. The whole camp staff and all the campers were in there worshiping on a hot night with the doors open, but there were devils and spirits trying to get us, and God had covered us with a supernatural protection so that they could not get in. God will protect you from whatever it is that you are experiencing. I understand that I am not the only person that has experienced this. I understand that there are people reading this right now that are saying, 'Sam, you don't understand the torment'. I understand that there are people who have been to church all their lives and have not been here; that does not mean that what you are experiencing is not *significant*, it is.

What you need to realise is that God gives us a dream. He plants that dream so deep in our heart that sometimes we cannot even see it. Sometimes, it takes maturity to draw the dream out, wisdom to understand the dream, and discernment to know it is from God. And what God does is he pulls us back. He pulls us as far away from the dream as possible, a bit like a bow and arrow.

When you pull the arrow back, you are setting it up to reach a target; you are giving it everything that it needs to be able to reach its destination, you are creating potential energy. And when you release that arrow, you cause a momentum. You cause the air in its way to be displaced, you cause kinetic energy. When you let go of that bow, *something has to change*!! You better realise that when God is pulling you back, it feels like the world is coming against you. The spiritual realm is on your case. The world is on your back. You are jailed. You are oppressed, ignored, belittled. You better believe that it is a setback and when God releases you into the destiny, the purpose, the potential he has given you, *things have to change!*!!

Things around you have to react to the name and the calling and the purpose of Jesus, because that is your AUTHORITY, your God given authority. *but*, we need to be teaching this to the people we are leading to the truth. We have to encourage them to press into who God says they are; who they are in Him and what he has given us. They have to be aware that we are at war.

Grace > The Enemy

CHAPTER 17

It's Solid, It's Liquid, IT'S OOBLECK!

I don't know how many of you ever made Oobleck in Science. I don't know why, but it is something that has stuck with me since making it. I could even tell you the colour of food colouring I used (red) and even the teacher that taught the class (Miss Bowes). *How cool is oobleck?* I hope you're feeling my excitement over something that can be both *solid* and *liquid*! Mind blowing right? You stir it and it's all gooey like slime. Then you hit it with quite a force and it's not budging. Like, "Nope, you're not getting in here." Too cool! Or maybe that is just the nerd in me.

Recently, we were talking with the youth at church about what it is they stand on when things go wrong. Following this, the topic cropped up more and more; in Home group, in personal conversations, and even in my own personal devotions. We say that God is our solid rock. We regurgitate scripture suggesting God is our solid rock, but is he really? And how do we know? What is it that we come right back to, that we reach out to help us, that we trust in when everything is on its head? But what do people who don't believe in our great and mighty God turn back to when they are wavering in strength? Why is it that sometimes we struggle with it being God? Why is it so difficult to depend on our creator? If your iPhone died, you would turn to apple to fix it. So why then, when life dies, do we not trust God to fix it?

I think a big part of this solid rock is prayer. I am convinced that some people genuinely think that God doesn't answer prayer. That he sits there like the judges on the X factor and pushes his great big 'no' buzzer when he doesn't want to answer a prayer. Like it's just discarded in a 'next' kind of attitude. I think people genuinely think God has to think about whether he's going to answer what we ask, as if it really troubles him. Like, "Ooh, I'll have to think about that." Come on people! What is this? *God always answers prayer*! Always! Like, without even thinking about it! There's no contemplation as to if he's going to answer what you ask of him. He already knows what you're going to ask, why would he need to think about it? Just because we don't get the answer we want doesn't mean we haven't gotten an answer. The bible says, "Ask and it will be given to you, seek and you shall find, knock and the door shall be opened." What are we saying? That Jesus was lying when he said those words after the most famous sermon ever? Yeah, I didn't think so either. God wants to stay in continual communion with us. He wants us to want him, and he wants us to focus on him. The issue is … are we listening? There is something powerful, so powerful, about the word that we speak into life. God creates when he speaks. He brings forth life. So what does that mean for the words we speak in prayer?

I had worked a full summer. It was my second summer at camp and personally my favourite, although it was also the most wild. I was due to return to the UK and start my Masters in Social Work. Instead, what happened was very different. Kelsey, who had worked at a different Camp in the states, had flown and met us in Chicago and we had all driven back to Ohio together. From here, we would go on to the airport to fly to NYC. As we ate chipotle and drove to the airport, it was like the last supper. This is always my last meal in America, because I absolutely love it and there aren't any over here. We laughed and cried and loved on each other. There was so much love in that van on the way to the airport. Yet again, I had decided I wasn't going to go back to Camp the summer after. By this point, you'd think I would have gotten the point from God, but I had said goodbye to everyone, including demike, and in my head, it was a final goodbye. I had come to the end of a chapter and as amazing and dreamlike as it had been whilst it had lasted, it was done, and I was letting go. I was like a child letting go of their balloon; sad and solemn, but knowing there was really nothing I could do about it. So with all this emotion and thought surging through me, and a constant refrain from acting out and blubbing everywhere, the whereabouts of my passport had not been a second thought for me, not even a consideration before I left. I knew I was totally organised and that it was in my purse … but was it? Never underestimate God's plan. It will always be more than you can think up or speak into life.

After pulling up at the airport and unloading our mountains of suitcases (three girls travelling in a different country requires a full wardrobe of clothes to be crammed so precisely into a suitcase), it suddenly hit me that I was not certain of where my passport actually was. I checked my handbag, it wasn't there. I checked my suitcase, it wasn't there either. The girls all checked their bags to be sure that none of them had it. So at this point, any normal person would have been freaking out. Kelsey and Fran were beyond freaking out. I, on the other hand, was as chilled as a snowflake. I had such an inner conviction of peace and I was literally not blown by this wind. I think I secretly always knew that God wanted me to stay in America. You know when God has planted something in your heart. I guess I was just unable to admit it to myself and other people, but God knew, and his plan was just about to unfold. After forcing Kelsey and Fran onto their flight to NYC without me, I got in the van with Jerome and Sarah, my

American friends whom I worked and lived with. The three of us experienced so much peace. I don't actually think I had ever experienced God's peace until this moment. It soaked deep within my soul. A peace that assured me that although this situation was slightly worrying, God was so in control. This summer, I had true revelation that God is alive and that he is at work, and this was a manifestation of that for me. He became very real that day in a tangible, supernatural kind of way. A way you cannot describe or ask anyone else to understand, but a way that you just know things are about to change massively.

Mid-journey home, Jerome looked at me and said, "I think we kind of get the picture that God wants you to stay in America now." And I am declaring that prophesy in my life!

Days and Days went by and I still had no passport, but I was certain that it would come when it was too late for me to get my flight back to the UK. Like God was preventing every possibility of me doing the things I had planned, and that I would have to step out in faith into his plan. One thing I was certain of, that it would show up after my flight left the states. During my time in the States, I stayed with Sarah and her family. It was so amazing to live within a family situation where they all love Jesus. It was a true example to me of how I want my family to be. How amazing it is when you declare, 'As for me and my house, we will serve the lord.' It was also so nice to just do life with one of the most amazing people, and be able to sit and talk to her day to day about things, opposed to having to do it via the internet or texts. We decorated her room. We went out to eat. We went to watch boys 2 men. We bible studied. We spent time with Amy and Jerome. It was one of the most refreshing times of my life. I must admit, one of my favourite parts of being in Marion was Pastor Rick. He has the most amazing revelation of the cross and is so Audacious about what he brings to the front of church. I learned a lot here about what it means to actually be a Christian. It was a time to be still and learn, to enter a new dimension, because when you step into something new, you have to sit back and learn.

The day after my flight left for the UK we found my passport on Sarah's bed side table, the bed we had been sleeping in the whole time … yeah, go figure!

During my time with the Simmons, I learned a lot about prayer. I think it may have been the first time I actually prayed properly - in my own daily routine and not just when I had to at church or camp, or when I felt like I needed to. It became a discipline, a part of who I am, and I actually didn't realise all that much. Prayer is such a journey. Breaking past that initial strange feeling and convincing yourself that you are not crazy for speaking to yourself, and that someone is actually listening. Or getting over being so open in front of people. Then, figuring out when to pray and what to pray. Do you pray scripture? Do you declare things or ask for them? My word, it is a journey! Think of some of the things that you have prayed for. I remember, in my second summer at camp, I prayed, for some insane reason, for 'Patience'. It is safe to say I will not be praying that one again! The best part of the journey of prayer is that God doesn't have an issue with answering it. Oh no, he enjoys answering it! He loves providing for his children! How beautiful is that? He tells us, just like an earthly parent, that he isn't going to give us a rock when we asked for bread. How truly beautiful! The hardest part about prayer is knowing that God doesn't always give us what we think we want. He actually gives us what he knows we need, and boy can that be tough. God loves the fact that we come to him so raw and honest, and at that moment in time, that is the truest version of ourselves. Prayer truly reveals our perspective of who we see God to be. It releases out faith for the impossible. I know that sometimes it can be an awful let down when someone goes somewhere else for something instead of coming to you, especially when you know you could have given them it. I can imagine that it is a bit like that with God. That he sits, as gentleman like as possible, saying that he will wait until we are done, knowing he has what we need.

What we declare in over our lives will come to fruition. If we say over and over again that we don't want something to happen, what is the likelihood that it will? The more we verbalise our fears and proclaim the brokenness for our lives, the more we will see it. Life and death is in the tongue, and the words you speak literally have a power beyond belief. This authority is given to us. It is a gift, not earned. We see it most beautifully when we Jesus, who is connected to the source, becomes our channel to our spirit and the Holy Spirit. And we receive what he is giving us. We allow him to come and work in and through us. The words you pray, the words you say, matter. They matter so much.

"You better build your house upon a rock. You need a good foundation on a solid spot. Oh the storms they come and go, but the peace of God you will know." That's a song that I sang in primary school. God's peace comes from him being the rock upon which we place our salvation. What does your prayer life truly say about who you believe God to be? Is He Solid, Liquid, or Oobleck?

Grace > Negative Declarations

CHAPTER 18

Just Hold On

Today is the first day I have sat down to write in an incredibly long time. The winds of life had swept me up so drastically that the things I love to do were brushed under the rug for no one to see. Although I was encouraged over the summer months to write, it just didn't feel quite right. Like I didn't have anything all that important to say. That what I did have was time to spend with people, time to invest into people, time to be around people, and to love on people. It was a people season. It was a season of doing opposed to reflecting. And I feel that reflecting is the best time to sit in the quiet and do something you love. You sit with gratitude, looking back over time that has moved so quickly. Enjoying every last moment that happened, as if it were just yesterday. Smelling the familiar smells and tasting the foods you enjoyed so much during those times, only in your imagination. It is something to be grateful for, and something that comes and goes with the hustle and bustle of life. It is often difficult for us to sit back and observe God's might and his magnificent blessings in our lives. I have said it once and I will say it again, hindsight is one of the biggest blessings. It allows us to look back and see where God has intervened so graciously in our worlds, in ways so intricate you wouldn't notice at the time. It's almost like a jeweller when he inspects a piece of beautiful jewellery. He sees things that our naked eye wouldn't originally see. He sees the hallmarks which indicate its value. He sees the wear and tear of everyday life, the times it has been scratched from hands being careless, and even broken and then repaired.

Right now, I am again in a season of wait and I find myself laughing under my breath at my Father in heaven as he shakes his head and says, "Sam, look … it could be easy if you just let go … Let go of that impatience. Let go of that control and just submit to me." God is all knowing like the jeweller and his piece of jewellery, and he is all able like the jeweller and his ability to see fine detail. The only way things will develop is if you face things head on. So again, I enter another great wait. Strength will rise as we wait upon the Lord. This one is significantly different to the last one. This one, I suppose, sometimes, I feel excited for. I feel a great peace about this new journey. It's like I'm floating downstream on a spring day, catching the beautiful rays of sunshine whilst the birds of the sky enjoy the good weather, and the insects come out in full force. The flowers and plants of the banks have multiplied drastically and threaten to take over the stream, whilst the fish dart about under the boat playing, it seems like children. In the distance, you can hear people laughing and children playing from the houses that meet the river bank sides. The distant smell of a cook-out, mixed with pollen of every kind, floating in the air like a potion. Every now and again, the current will get a little strong and you will have to recalculate the direction of the boat, or move for an oncoming rock or tree. But all in all, the general journey is smooth. Obviously, the point of the journey is to reach your destination. Be it; to have a break and sit down, and enjoy your surroundings and even maybe some food, or to reach home and start a new journey. Nevertheless, you just soak up the journey. You notice every little smell and noise along the way, and you absorb it all into your memory. This is a journey I am looking forward to.

This time around, God has offered me a sense of security I never would have imagined. He offered me the promise of love. The promise that even though I have done this journey before, this time, it is going to be different. This time is going to be special and beautiful in very different ways to the other journeys I have been on.

Demichael Lewis Nelson proposed to me in front of the people who are important to us on the 1st of August in 2013. This was one of the happiest days of my life to date. Obviously, every woman who has been asked to spend the rest of her life with the man she is in love with can say the same. That day, I was no longer a habitant of Earth as we know it. I was floating away in some other dimension. This was a day I had dreamed of for a very long time. A day I had prayed for for a very long time. However, it had only ever been a dream. Life was against Demichael and me. Being from different countries and having families who were not in extreme wealth means the past three years of our lives have been incredibly difficult. We have spent long periods of time away from each other, yearning the touch, the smell, and the voice of one another. But God blessed me with a dream that has so drastically changed my life, and thus allowing me to trust, even more, that God always has a plan, and that behind the curtains of our reality, and behind the scenes of this thing that we call life, God is working. Working mightily to bless us with the desires of our hearts. To provide us with an eternal joy. He is constantly changing the circumstances in our lives for times of redemption and breakthrough. This was a day of breakthrough ... for the both of us. Breakthrough of circumstances holding us back. Breakthrough of finding love in all the wrong places. Breakthrough of living a lonely existence. Breakthrough of history. And breakthrough that God promises us that we don't have to live out our parents' lives again. That we are created to make our own future, that is very specific to us.

That our future doesn't have to look like anyone else's, because it is so specifically designed for us. To be so individual to whom we are and not where we have come from. Deciding to say yes to Demichael was the easiest and most amazing decision (after following Jesus) I have made.

However, as often as fortune falls in our laps, misfortune or discomfort does also. Not everyone is happy about the things that make you happy. Not everyone knows the journey you have been on. Therefore, not everyone understands the breakthrough you are experiencing. Lack of connection to a situation can often bring around negative reactions. Lack of emotional attachment to a situation also does the same. So when announcing our engagement, not everyone was rushed off to our perpetual state of dream land. They were stuck very firm on earth, on their piece of soft land. Be it jealousy, be it confusion or doubt, or even worry; they didn't find themselves in the breakthrough that we had found ourselves in. They didn't see our situation from our own, or from God's, perspective. I am a firm believer that God will take the least likely of people and create a significant story. He will take people who are not able, who are defiant, detested, and destructive and make a beautiful love story of how much he loves his people. A love story about how he is the most devoted father. He will work through their weakness. He doesn't count up our strengths when he wants to use us. Instead, he looks at how he can be glorified, because it is in his strength alone. Thus none of us can boast. It is about how great he is and him unaided. Our situation does not define whether or not God will use us. Everyone is usable, but it is whether we will allow God to use us.

When Demichael and I first met, we were far from the man and woman of God that we have grown into. In fact, at the time, we were both fighting with the fact that there is a God out there who is very much alive and who very much loves the entirety of our being. We were struggling with the concept of giving up the things that we put our love into. I lived in a situation where I loved God, but I enjoyed sinning too much to commit anything to anyone; to the extreme where I was given Kyle Idleman's book, *Not a Fan* and put off reading it for almost two years, because I knew the content and that God would challenge me on the fact that sinning was still too attractive, too enjoyable, too fun for me to stop. Boy was I wrong! So this has been a very out stretched journey, and at times, both of us have felt like an elastic band waiting to snap. But the Holy Spirit often comes and reminds us that it is all in God's perfect timing and that his plan is, and will be, better than anything we could possibly hope for or imagine, or even string together in our own minds. As I look back over the past years together and the struggle and the hurt we have been through, and have put each other through, I am thankful for a multitude of things. I am thankful that all the things that happened encouraged us to not only grow as individuals and grow together, but it encouraged us to reach out to God, to reach out to his eternal out stretched hand, and to accept his undeserving gift of grace. People suggest that good things come to those who wait and the best things come to those who are patient, but I think that the most important things come to those who are willing to fight for them. Those who are passionate enough to not let go, to not cease to care. Those who have a fire deep within them that won't let them just sit and wait, or sit around patiently waiting for life to happen. They make a Decision. When I think about the word passion, I think of lots of things. Mostly, successful people who have poured themselves into something that they are passionate about. I think about hobbies, and I think about *dreams*. Being passionate about something is an emotion that is so powerful, it is barely containable. It is hard to put a lid on a passion, like bees in a jar. It is hard to contain. When you think about passionate emotions, you think of love most of all, but you think of excitement and joy, as well as negative emotions such as hatred or anger. These all derive from a passion about something or someone. Have you ever been so passionately excited that you cannot contain your enthusiasm and all you want to do is share this feeling with other people? It's all you talk about and all you think about, and you even go to the extreme of trying to fit this passion into every conversation you have. When you look at the definition of 'Passion', you will often find them talk about the suffering and death of our saviour Jesus. This, I think, is something phenomenal that the actual definition of passion is made up of the suffering of Jesus. That is our ultimate example of passion, a passion for people, and a passionate lover. There is no passion to be found in settling for a life that is less than what you deserve, or are capable of with God. Jesus didn't settle for anything less than dying for his people, so we shouldn't die for anything less than what we are passionate about. Passion tells you to *fight*. Fight for what you believe in. Fight for what you want. Fight for the change you want to see. Fight for the people who have forgotten how to fight. Make the decision to fight, because you best believe that the devil is fighting. He is fighting for the truth and love and breakthrough not to come to fruition. What he puts in your life to set you back, God is using to set you up. Keep on fighting! Change your perception. You are not defeated or a victim. You are victorious! You are the head and not the tail, because he will give you a thought that warps your perception to change. You can become self-seeking and destructive in the space of one thought. Every action starts as a thought. You are in control of your thoughts and you are worthy. Although it pains me to say now, there has been a point where both Demike and I have felt punished by God, felt ignored and forgotten about. This has been a journey we have both been on together. Allowing ourselves to live under other people. Feeling ourselves, and our relationship, unworthy. This is not truth though. We felt punished in regard to having to go through another length of time away from each other, and only viewing it as a negative experience. These things are just us missing the touch of God. In reality, we are just not seeing the touch of God. God tells us he is Emmanuel, 'God with us'. He is constant and faithful – meaning he is always with us, always blessing us. It is just up to us to see and feel his touch. It is important for us to realise that happiness is just a mood, not a destination. It is a journey, not a final point. I have learned the hard way that this is a transition, a journey, a way of life. Eternity is our destination. It is our decision to ignore, or overlook, Gods touch in our lives. I am learning more and more how much of a gentleman he is. I often saw this time away from Demike, missing all these things, as negative. However, as time has gone by and I have looked over the things. I have been praying for our relationship, for our marriage, that we are strong and wise. What better way to strengthen a couple than to put them on opposite sides of the planet and ask them to function? God is an incredibly gentle and loving God and now I view my time away very differently.

I have spent a lot of time recently planning our wedding. It is some time away and, as it stands, it is currently hanging in the balance of a visa, but I still have hope. I have hope to see my plans come to pass, so I plan and dream and imagine, and yeah, sometimes it scares me. It scares me to think that I have to execute a wedding. It scares me that it won't all go to plan. It scares me that it won't be the most perfect magical day that I imagine it to be inside my brain. But I still plan in hope that I will one day get to wear a dress and feel like a princess whilst I say, 'I do' in front of all the people that we care about and care about us. Whilst planning the things I have planned, I have faced a lot of questions … What colours, which dress, will that neckline suit everyone, what about if people don't like the taste of that, and all sorts of things I didn't think I would ask myself. What I did find myself asking was, *what does marriage mean to me? What does a wedding mean to me? What does this decision of commitment mean to me?* They both mean very different things to me. Marriage means a lifetime to me. Marriage is something I was created for, something God designed me to do, a decision I will make every day to love someone. A wedding is a day, one day, that happens in your life; that doesn't define you or your marriage. It doesn't change things or enhance things. It is a day you decide that you are making a commitment under God, in front of the people that you love, to be there for someone 'till death do us part'. So do all the other things that a wedding has been made about really matter? Does it have to be a fairy tale, or does it just have to be real? Real life truth.

Be bold enough to use your voice, the one God has given you to use, to impact people with. Be brave enough to follow your heart. God speaks to your heart. It is where everything flows from. And be strong enough to live the life you have always imagined, because there is only you in control of that. It is hard to see strength within yourself when you face challenges of life, when you feel weak. These past few days, I have felt weak. I have explained to Demike how I currently feel spent, like there isn't much left to give, but I am still holding on. When you are passionate about something, it doesn't matter how little energy you have left, it is impossible to let go. I believe that God sent you, Demichael, into my life. To give me something to fight for. To be passionate about. To show me that, in this world, there is love. To give me hope and to bring me joy, and sometimes pain. And to show me that God is for me. You were a gift from the heavens. I know that we are going to come out the other side stronger, as we have the realisation of things that we are incredibly thankful for. And this is God's touch, God's passion.

Today, I sit down to write. The winter months are vast upon us and the cold has crept in like the tide on a summer day. Without actual realisation that something is changing, you just awake one day to the change. The nights are long. It is dark when I leave for work and dark when I return home. It makes me want to curl up in front of the fire and keep warm and snug all day. It's a time of the year where I love long walks, all wrapped up in all kinds of miss-match woollen clothing, just to feel toasty. The time of year where the days are so crisp and fresh, where everything has died or hibernated for the winter, and although it sounds sad, like things have come to end, it is actually beautiful. It is beauty in its purest form. The crisp crumpled leaves that litter the floor and the naked trees that pollute the skyline. Everything in this season can become bitter sweet. It can be tiresome dragging yourself out of bed to face the darkness. It can be tough to miss the beauty of daylight, and to not be able to snuggle all day, or take day long walks. But as with everything that comes with the season, if you let it, it can spiral out of control, into a state of despair; yearning for the warm touch of the sun, wanting and craving the rays to dance across your skin. Today, this has reminded me of what it is like when I distance myself from God. Sometimes, I find myself plodding through life, facing things on my own, believing in myself that I can do it, and I catch myself yearning, craving, wanting something more. It isn't long before I realise that, in reality, this thing that I am craving never actually left. I realise that God is our source of life and we need to be in constant connection with that. It isn't that we get up one day and decide, *oh, today I am going to behave like Jesus.* It is that we are so connected to our source that, out of us, flows Jesus. That his characteristics manifest within our hearts, and that is how we behaved without even thinking about it all that much. We are so connected to God that it is second nature to follow the Spirit's prompting. It was there all along. God never leaves us. He never forsakes us. I am really enjoying just being consumed by life right now. I am enjoying being pulled up into the arms of a routine and being able to get up every day and know what's going to happen. Although

I do moan a considerable amount, this structure gives you time to be able to consider a lot of factors in your life – being in the midst of the season can be time to contemplate what it is that is going on around you. I am currently working for the government, of which I have found difficult. It has been tough getting up every day to not feel like you are going to change someone's life in your day. Not have an impact on their lives or change their way of thinking. Or that is what I had told myself; that the job I was in didn't serve all that much purpose to anything really. But it is me that has to remind myself that every situation we are in is a mission field, and we have to have faith in the things that are unseen. We do not know what is going on behind the front that we see from the people whom we come into contact with every day. I don't want to have to yearn for those things, for the soft kiss of change, for the incitement of something different. I want to be understanding what it is that is going on, because true happiness is not a destination, it is a journey. It is where you are right now. It is enjoying the fragility of life, the fact that we aren't promised another day, and enjoying the day we are in.

Knowing that each and every day has a multitude of blessings within it. This is something that I am learning more and more as I mature; that it is ok for me to be happy, to enjoy the life that I am living. Although it isn't quite my dream, I am not going to get there overnight, and that I have to wake up every day and work towards the happiness that I so often dangle in front of myself, like a carrot on a stick. It doesn't mean that I am not fighting to be better and for better. It just means that I know how sacred life is, and how this can be taken from us within the blink of an eye. I am the person that is in charge of my own happiness. I find my strength in Jesus, but I am the person who decides if I see things as a blessing or a misfortune. Our perception is key.

I have also realised that I am a person that lives by emotion. I am consumed and controlled by my feelings. They lead me like a great dictator, and this can be very dangerous for me, and often leads to frustration and heartbreak. I am called to be led by someone who is greater than emotions, and I am called to be in control of my own life, not to be controlled by aspects of it. This is very like the winter months. We can view it as a cold bitter season, but in reality it is so much more. So I decide every day to draw closer to God, and guess what? I have literally seen him draw closer to me. I see the cross.

Grace > Giving up

CHAPTER 19

Decisions, Decisions, Decisions

You can't have a beautiful ending without making mistakes, or so I hear. I have made a few mistakes. I wouldn't quite call them beautiful, but they have shaped me. Everyone makes them. Each one has a different effect on our lives and what happens from that moment on. Some are brushed under the rug and buried in the past, some are never forgiven and brought up every day like the sun from the depths of the East, but they all have one important point. They remind us what it is that is important to us, what it is that matters, that makes us. They cause us to stop in this hectic rush of life and think, *was it worth it really?* Even 'little' mistakes can make us stop in our tracks and question ourselves of our motives.

For as long as there is hope, there is no fear. I constantly find myself in situations recently where I have previously stated, and I quote, "If I was in that situation, I would do this ..." Well, guess what? I haven't done what I had previously stated I would. I have, in fact, done the complete opposite. It is easy for us to allow our morals and ideals for life to be held up by standards, by other people's standards. It's nice, sometimes, to think of yourself as the 'strong independent' person that would walk away, or do the 'right thing'. However, what I'm realising more and more is that those situations where I stated I would do the 'right/strong/independent' thing, really, none of those things were particularly strong. Anyone can say that they are going to behave in a particular way, but someone who behaves in a way that is true to their heart, and true to what makes them them, is a strong person.

In life, if you let it, you can always come up with reasons to let go and walk away. More often than not, we view that as a strong idea, especially when discussing what we would do in certain situations. But really, if you don't and you cling on for dear life, then you might just find love in places that you never imagined. Even if you don't give up, you just might find something that you never thought possible. But you also might find a strength that you didn't realise you had. When it comes to the day that we are going to leave this earth, are we going to look back and think, *I am glad I made that decision*, or are we going to look back and think, *In that situation, I loved with all that I am, and it grew and changed me to become a better person, who could, therefore, love with everything that makes me?*

I think when we face decisions regarding issues in our lives, the easy thing is to walk away, but it isn't just as simple as walking away. We are human beings who thoroughly enjoy protecting ourselves. We use defence mechanisms to prevent the gut wrenching feeling of hurt. So when we walk away, each time raises the standard of expectation for the next person, or even the same person. It is unrealistic for us to presume that anyone walking this earth is, or has, the capacity to be perfect. There once was one, but the bible tells us he is now seated at the right hand of God in a place that we can only dream of right now. However, something I am having issues with currently is taking people as they are and keeping that standard throughout our relationship. They were enough for me to initially love in my mind, so this should be the standard throughout the relationship. Then also, finding that balance that even though I am committed,

I don't want to be absolutely taken for a ride, because I am a Christian. There is a fine line between mistake and injustice, and in reality, only you can make the call. It is also a testament to the fact that the barriers you keep putting up. God will keep trying to pull down. God's love for us is limitless, relentless, and perfect, and I know that it is not possible for us to love like he does, but because he does love, we can too.

As we get to know people, as we delve into the depths of which they are, as we share hurt and joy, and even food with them, we develop a whole new level of respect. This, in turn, raises our standard bar for them. And this is unfair. Everyone, at some point in our lives, is going to hurt us. Some people may repeatedly do so. A lot of the time, this is unintentional. People don't truly understand the consequences to their actions until they are living in them, but we are called to keep the same standard. We hold expectations for people that are not only unrealistic, but unfair. It is unrealistic that someone can protect our hearts greater than God. This comparison astounds me! No one will ever do that, and no one will ever be able to protect our hearts in a way we want them to. Not even ourselves. We know ourselves, how difficult it can be, sometimes, to be a human, and when we think if we could protect someone's heart, the overwhelming sense of responsibility is enough to say, "No, I can't do it." We were created to be selfish, that is our sinful fleshly downfall, and as much as we like to think we could, it is impossible. Sometimes, it is just inevitable that your partner/ friends/associates' needs will be overlooked, whether it be on purpose or by accident.

I know that right now, there are people close to me, in my life, including my husband, that will hurt me. I often find that I am offended, because people do not think the way that I do, or would. However, they will hurt me in some way. That doesn't mean that I should pack up and leave, because they do so. It means, I am about to face an important decision, in regard to which path I take next. It means that I am going to take it to God and remind myself that those people and situations are not my problem. All I can do is stay true. I cannot, and I will not, take it into my own hands to change people, but I will tolerate more than people think is acceptable, and forgive more than people think is actually reasonable, and love more than people actually think possible. Because I know who I am, and I know the God I serve.

Forgiveness is something that we wake up and do continually – the bible tells us that God's mercies are new every day. And although we probably have things that we need forgiveness for everyday, God forgives over and over again. This is something we should discipline ourselves to do. Even if every hour of everyday we need to remind ourselves that we need to forgive someone for something. It is a decision and a discipline that can be very difficult, but totally worth it. Unforgiveness is like carrying a bag of cement around with us. It is draining, and ultimately pointless. However, forgiveness is not our only decision – love is a decision. It is up to us to choose to love people, no matter where they are in their walk. We may be overwhelmed with a sense of 'in love', but to love someone is a decision.

Relationships, if anything else, are a commitment. A commitment to discipleship and to be obedient to what God has called us to do. A commitment to love. A commitment to put someone else before yourself. All this may sound very profound, but in reality, we have to work towards all good things. Nothing good ever comes easy, and what would be the point in that anyway? Would we feel the same sense of good? Or would we get bored and eventually give up? Would we realise and see our blessings of God's faithfulness? Decide to love.

I have been making a lot of big decisions recently, in regard to lots of things … Where we want to live, where I want to work, what to buy people for Christmas, what I want for my lunch … Some have a bigger impact on my life than others, but nevertheless, they all impact me in some way, shape, or form. The decisions I make all say something about me. About who I am and how I am hardwired. What makes me tick. What I value. What my downfalls are. Who I listen to. What kind of a God I serve. Even the smaller decisions give people an image of what kind of person I am. Those larger decisions take a little more time mulling over. They require me to check that one scripture just that one more time. They make me question myself – make me question my ideals and my morals, and make me wonder, *If I do this, what kind of person would I be?* They make me want to understand who I was created to be that little bit more. They make me realise, more and more, how I want my actions to be seen. I want them to be seen as a response to the gospel.

Last night, I brought in the New Year in a way I never had before – sober with friends. It was like something I have never experienced, but it was so what I needed. I couldn't even begin to put into words. Whilst working at camp, I have met people that are my brothers and sisters in Christ. It is like we have opened secrets together and have this unique bond that only we understand, that only we appreciate and love. It is something so special and unique, and something I am incredibly thankful for, as well as something that I cannot explain. Ask anyone who has worked at Jesus camp. You are passionate about the relationships you made there. One relationship that I made at camp was like no other, and I am certain that everyone he is friends with will tell you the same. Nathan Flynn is unique in so many ways. I don't know that anyone has an average relationship with this guy. He is uniquely Irish, he is uniquely a follower of Christ, and he is uniquely funny. And he legitimately mistook a frog for a scorpion. He often even sings about horses. He is someone I admire greatly! His sense of humour always has me laughing, and I appreciate his company like the honey bee appreciates honey … a lot!

It was the first time we had actually spent time together in the UK. He studies in America and I am often between the countries, so more often than not, he will meet me stateside and we will discuss life beyond the pond, that at times seems like a distant fairytale. He invited myself and Kelsey to go up to his brother's house in Newcastle and spend the night. Although apprehensive about what would occur, I was excited to be surrounded by people who love Jesus, and this would be a first for me, for the New Year. Midnight came in and we were surrounding a handmade fire, watching the fireworks go off in the distance. It was humbling to know that I am a new creation and that people do love me for who I am, and that I do make a difference and I am loved by people. It also had me thinking about New Years and what they actually mean. It's always just an excuse for people to try and make a change and to try and do something different. Maybe they feel guilty about the excessive amounts of food and alcohol they have consumed in such a short period of time. Maybe they had to squeeze into their New Year outfit. Who knows … but there's always the usual resolutions suggested here, there, and everywhere. This prompted me to think what mine would be. What would inspire me this year to change? What was it that I wanted to change exactly? And I thought about my relationships and my family, and God, and I realised that I don't want to change. Not one thing. My God is the same yesterday, today, and tomorrow; meaning, he is all I need. I don't need a fad diet or to stop excess to know that I am loved. I need MORE. More of a perfect God. More of an ever present God. More of a providing loving God. It's not change that I want, it's more. More heaven here on earth! More miracles! More blessings, and more breakthroughs. I want my dreams to scare me. I want to believe the impossible will happen. This year, I am going to believe for more and dream bigger dreams.

I have seen this already … God is a faithful God, and when he says he is going to do something, he does it. Recently, I have been very caught up in the parable in Luke and Matthew about the five Loaves and the two Fish. I've been just so amazed and astounded by what actually happens here. These disciples have been out in the villages on mission, just like we would. They have been preaching and healing and seeing miracles. They get back and all they want to do is chill out. They have been without money and living off people for ages, and they just want a good meal and to kick it with each other. Then, as always, Jesus causes a crowd. Jesus and his radical way of living cause the masses to gather. Something that always crosses my mind is, *why?* I mean I know how amazing Jesus is. I know in my heart how much I love him, and that is because of all the amazing things he has done, and continues to do for me. But it's also because the bible tells me. There has to have been something about the way that Jesus lived and the way he did things. Maybe, there was just something slightly magnetic about him that encouraged people to draw to him, to draw close to him. I just often sit and think why this might be? This is the thought that spurs me to live like him. To live in such a radical way that people turn their heads and think, "I want what she has." I have started to question myself about how to approach the lost. How is it best to draw alongside them and introduce them to Jesus? I have tried the preaching. I've tried the 'not really mentioning anything but being there' approach. Neither have really seemed to cause a radical response. It was when I read the passage in Matthew 14 that I realised that all I need to do is live like him. To mirror the way he behaved and what he believed. There must have been so much conviction in the words he spoke, in the way he held himself, in the look in his eyes, that it was enough for people to want to listen to what he had to say. To want to continue on his journey with him. To understand and appreciate that he is the son of God. This really just blows my mind!

I have also been astounded by God's approach to the crowds, and the food and the disciples. I know now that when camp is over, all I want to do is to eat and sleep, and just relax. Mission can be so draining. So these disciples, who have been gone for however long, must want nothing more than to chill out. But there isn't much chance of that when you hang with Jesus. There can't be much quiet time to yourself (unless of course you are spending it with God). Hence why they asked Jesus to just send them into town to feed themselves. I can imagine they were just waiting for them to leave so that they could catch up on rest. Jesus had other ideas, knowing fine well that there was nowhere near enough food to be able to feed them, but he knew, and trusted, the one he served would provide in an instant. The part that really comforts me is that when the disciples suggested all they had was two fish and five loaves, Jesus replied, "Bring them to me." As if it was no issue whatsoever! God knows all we have to offer, and he is such a loving and compassionate God, that it is enough. What we have to offer him is enough, and he will always add more. He always has something to add to us. When we bring him all that we have, he can do the most amazing miracles. He wants us to realise what he can do through us and with us. What we have is enough, and there is nothing too little to offer to the kingdom of God. What we do have to do is make the decision to keep pressing on. When we have no energy or drive and all we have to offer is two measly loaves and a few fish with countless hands reaching out to be fed. When the future seems impossible, and you literally cannot make that step forward. You do not know how you will make it. DO IT! Keep pressing forward and watch what happens when you decide to trust.

The last thing that amazes me, and really shows me God's goodness, is that even after all this, the disciples still had their fill.

There is no coincidence that there were twelve leftover baskets. That's one basket each. They had enough, and some. And this, I see as reward. Reward for what they had done. And a reminder that nothing ever goes unnoticed. God is a truly good God, but I guess when I prayed for more crazy in my life, I didn't actually realise how crazy it would get.

Grace > Making the wrong decision

CHAPTER 20

A blank page

Someone once told me that I was a foolish Christian and that I only followed Jesus for the benefits but was not willing to accept the persecutions and suffering trials that we were also called to take joy in. At the time, I was more than offended and jumped to defend myself. How could someone accuse me of such a thing? How could someone think that they have any kind of right to define my relationship with Jesus? How could someone possibly know what happens when I am with God? I spent some time offended, but it was quickly brushed under the rug, not to be acknowledged again, for a short time; another addition to the Pandora's Box of issues yet to be dealt with but likely to arise again in the future. Only they were to grow in size and become more deadly.

To this day, it was festering in its box with its friends of issues, but it wasn't until I looked back over the past year that I had actually realised that God, himself, had been dealing with it behind the scenes. The bible tells us that it is by grace we are saved in faith. This initial faith to believe is something that we have been prompted to by the Holy Spirit, but the bible also tells us that God gives us faith and that faith comes from the word. I genuinely believe that, over time, God will use the word to speak Faith into your life. Into your situation, into your circumstances, and into your expectations without you even realising. Until you reach that moment where you receive conviction and God removes yet another piece of wool from your eyes, and you view it how he wants you to view it, and you feel how he feels, and you understand what he wants you to understand, in the time he wanted you to understand it. It is about the Gospel living in and through you, and that becoming the life you lead, and I literally cannot explain this to you. I can try. The past twenty chapters are evidence of that, but I cannot explain the transformation that I have seen in my own life and in my own heart.

I have just started a new season, a new chapter of my book. After turning the page, and in lots of different ways, the cheek on a situation that had been so bittersweet, it has become apparent to me that God is my refuge. That he is my shelter on a dark stormy night. That he is my shack in the woods, in the rain. That he is my cave in the mountain from the thunder. That he is my tree in the meadow from the beaming sun. And that he has instilled this into my heart by showing his beautiful faithfulness through and through – and also how this is something that just happened, and how unaware of this I actually was. I say over and over and over again that hindsight is such an amazing blessing. We learn so much about the ways of God and the way he has worked with us personally, and charmingly, he makes beautiful things out of dust

Today is one year from the day I said, "I do". It is my first ever wedding anniversary and I did not think that I would be spending it like this. I wish I had the time and space to tell you every little detail of the past year to show you just how truly faithful God is, but all I can do is give you an overview and ask you to 'taste and see that the Lord is good'. I found out, this past year, that for the second time in marriage, my husband had been with another woman outside of the covenant that we had made under God, the Holy promise that our family had witnessed, the words that had been so unspoken but shown in actions. Right now, I expect you are waiting for me to tell you how my life turned upside down and how I was destroyed and it has been so difficult for me to come to terms with the situation, and other perilous thoughts and actions along those lines. If I did say those things, for the most part, they would not be true. Due to human nature, this is true for my initial reaction. Sometimes, I feel that when we first find out something catastrophic or life changing, something so human takes over us. It's like the fight or flight instinct that we seem to have no way to be able to tame it, to the point that we forget anything about the spirit of God that dwells within us, that is for us, and there to help us, that is fighting the Good fight with us. It's like the animal instinct comes out and we, all too often, want to react, opposed to act. This was me. Although not once throughout this whole situation have I said anything out of turn or raised my voice, at this point, I have to bury my pride and remind myself that it is by God alone that I am able to face this situation so humbly with such peace and grace in my heart. My actions still would not define the 'norm' for finding out this kind of endeavour had been occurring, but that is because God had blessed me with a Faith, an assurance, that he is in control. A peace that surpasses human understanding. A conscious awareness of his divinity and Lordship, not only over the situation or my life, but over humanity. And that's not even the start of it.

Satan was defeated – he will forever be defeated. Since the fall, he has become the prince of this earth, but that does not come with a victory. It doesn't come with honour or assurance that his will he conjures up for us has certainty in our lives. It comes with a forced white flag, a forced knee bowing to the name of Jesus. A forced knee bowing to the triumph of the cross and everything it stands for, which ultimately is not a life of fear but of freedom. Not a life of condemnation but of eternal life. Not a life of defeat and depression but of victory and joy. As the days pass, I realise more and more that this is God's will. That God has most certainly put me exactly where he wants me to be in life, and the same is true for you. The day after I found out about Demichael, my friend led a bible study at camp. Dave Webb, what a guy! He has to be one of the most incredible human beings I know. If you don't know him, find out who he is and get to know him. Everyone needs a Dave Webb. Camp is where I escaped to after the shocking realisation of truth. When I say he led it, I mean I most certainly took over. With an assurance of peace and spirit in my heart, we talked about Jesus and his plans for our lives, and how hurt comes into the situation. We just so happened to stumble across John 15:

"I am the true vine, and my Father is the gardener. 2 He cuts off every branch in me that bears no fruit, while every branch that does bear fruit he prunes[a] so that it will be even more fruitful. 3 You are already clean because of the word I have spoken to you. 4 Remain in me, as I also remain in you. No branch can bear fruit by itself; it must remain in the vine. Neither can you bear fruit unless you remain in me. 5 "I am the vine; you are the branches. If you remain in me and I in you, you will bear much fruit; apart from me you can do nothing. 6 If you do not remain in me, you are like a branch that is thrown away and withers; such branches are picked up, thrown into the fire and burned. 7 If you remain in me and my words remain in you, ask whatever you wish, and it will be done for you. 8 This is to my Father's glory, that you bear much fruit, showing yourselves to be my disciples. 9 "As the Father has loved me, so have I loved you. Now remain in my love."

Oh how true this is to our lives! God is continually weeding and pruning the dead vines in our lives. He is continually attracting us to move forward one step at a time. Just because we are exactly where he wants us to be does not mean that he wants us to stay there. Nothing that stays in the same place is encouraging. It becomes stagnant and nothing that is stagnant is good. It becomes a smelly, dirty, infectious state that is most certainly avoided. The things that he has placed in our lives can do the same. As humans, we are so very blessed with free will. What kind of a God we would serve if every decision was forced by him opposed to influenced and guided by him. He is such a true definition of 'Gentleman'. He knows the state of every heart. He knows the choices we make, and he most certainly knows what is best for us. God knows that by Demichael's free will, he had become stagnant. Stagnant to the point of falling back, the point of infection, and becoming contagious to those that surrounded him. That was his free will, to not follow the prompting of the spirit, to not stay true to the real Lord of his life, but to find victory and satisfaction in the destruction that the Prince of this world had offered him. He knows that I wasn't behaving like a wife. That, in our situation, we were drowning each other, and that it wasn't healthy. He also knew that we would both separately draw near to God and he would take us on a journey we couldn't even begin to imagine.

It wasn't until God had stripped everything from me that I realised the position I had been in. I had been a 'tomorrow' Christian. As in, *Maybe tomorrow, I will commit that to God. Maybe tomorrow, I will go on a mission. Maybe tomorrow, my husband and I will study the word together. Maybe tomorrow, God can have that part of my life.* Sometimes, God has to take you back to the vine for you to realise that you are not being who you committed yourself to be, who he created you to be. Jesus calls his followers and means for them to leave when he does. He doesn't call them and suggest it's fine when they are ready. What we don't realise as Christians is that this seems like an inconvenience, but it is God's perfect plan for an amazing life for us – a full life. Jesus came so that we could have life to the fullest, and that starts when we decide to follow him. Fully Follow Him! "The Land of tomorrow is where you find divorce, addiction, and unmanageable debt. The land of tomorrow is where you will find unfaithful spouses and prodigal children." – Kyle Idleman. For people, there is always an excuse to stay in a situation that is convenient for them. For Demike, it was convenient for him to behave the way the people surrounded him behaved. It was convenient for him to lie and cover up his mistakes. It was also convenient to tell himself, *Maybe tomorrow, I will try harder. Maybe when I get a visa, I will try harder. Maybe tomorrow, I will read my bible, go to church, and press into God's promises.* 'Maybe tomorrow' was too late for him, but 'maybe tomorrow' was the seed that God had planted to speak to him. Of this, we are all guilty. Although our consequences may not be as destructive of others, it is common for fear to encourage us to live in the Land of tomorrow. But Fear and Faith do not coincide. You live in one or you live in the other, and the decision of which is yours alone. No way am I putting it all on Demike. We all have our 'maybe tomorrows'. I had more than I can count … this book for one. And sometimes, God puts us in a situation where 'maybe tomorrow' is no longer an option, because we have to act now.

It was in Demike's 'maybe tomorrow' that I found I had been doing the same. Obviously not to the extent of the above, however, in the extent of 'Where you Go, I will go'. For the longest time, I have wanted to volunteer and go on a mission, and do all these things where I reach out to people. My excuses were always, "Maybe tomorrow, I will look into it. Maybe when Demike gets here, I will act upon it." … Always just empty promises to myself and to God. Make tomorrow your today. God will plant a dream in your heart and, in your due time, it will come to fruition. However, that can only come by actions and not by wishful thinking.

No one, apart from God himself, can force someone to change, and God loves his people so much that he would never do such a thing. He will provide our every need to be able to change, but the actions come from us and our hearts. He never puts us in situations of temptation without providing what we need to get out, and he never starts something good and leaves it unfinished. There, lies our hope. Hope that the people who choose destruction, and un-fulfilling promises from the Enemy, will find hope – that the seeds once planted will grow little by little into something so beautiful. The Truth. What I have realised over this past year is that everything, apart from me, is not my problem. Yes, we are called to act and to show Jesus, but we are not called to change people. That is God's problem. Demichael Lewis Nelson is God's problem, and not mine. I cannot fix him. I cannot change the way he thinks. I cannot change the way he acts. I cannot change how he feels or how he perceives. All I can do is declare goodness, truth, hope, and fullness over his life.

There were moments when there was a tight feeling in my chest. I am certain it was not because I was upset, or should I say regretful about what happened. It was probably more to do with the fact that I face the hurt daily and reality of things each day. I have found so much growth, peace, and encouragement in this hurt. It doesn't hurt nowhere near as much as it probably should without the grace of God. It's strange … it's so strange. Even if a relationship was so negative and sucked the life out of you, even if it was a relief to have left, even if you are moving on with life, it's strange that you grieve that person. It is like their negative impact in your life had such a hold on you that as much as it is liberating to let go, you now almost feel empty, or lonely. Like you are now left with a void to fill, time to occupy, and a whole lot of love to give. I have contemplated getting another animal. However, our house is so much like a zoo now, there isn't all that much room for any more animals, or human beings for that matter. But I think it would help just finding something to love on, something to do passionately and enjoy. That is what a relationship is, raw love and passion for another person with so much desire to see them happy, and to see them succeed and be everything they were created to be – to share all that you have to give with them. It is more of a blessing than we realise. Human beings like to know that people need them. Not only that they need them, that they appreciate them and the things that they do. Don't get me wrong, although my marriage turned incredibly sour for a period of time, I did receive that reinforcement to a certain extent. But now, I need to find new ways to serve my love to other people, and that has left me feeling hurt and with too many options I guess. So I guess the time we spent separate in the past year, has served the most amazing purpose.

The thing that I struggled with the most was that I just really didn't want to have to think about Demichael. It was not out of bitterness or resentment, but more just the fact that I thought I was totally willing and 'ready' to move on with my life. I didn't want his name to enter my brain and I didn't want to think about him when I woke up. I didn't want to check my phone for texts from him, or look on his Facebook page for his life updates. I didn't even want to see pictures of him. But I did. This wasn't out of me yearning him and his presence in my life, like God and the lost. It was more out of habit. It was more of a bad habit generated over time, but this had gotten me thinking about all my other bad habits. Waiting on Demike was a habit created that left me hungry. Hungry for something to pour all this love out onto. However, if the situation had not changed, I would not have realised that I had implemented this into my life. What else do I do this with in my life? Where else could I induce a hunger to serve by removing something unhealthy from my life? I guess I am understanding, more and more, why God suggests he wants all of us. Not just half, and not just a little bit, because those things that we keep from him are then held in the dark. They're not necessarily based on God's truth. Giving it to God means that we are allowing his good and perfect will – the truth to decode the cipher we once based our 'truth' on.

The more time has passed and the more quotes I read and the more pastors I hear speak and the more scripture I dive into, the more I come to the conclusion that we can convince ourselves that something is true when it isn't. Something as fundamental as love, we can confuse for lust. Peace, we can confuse for suppression. It's actually quite terrifying to think that the structure and foundations of our lives can be based on things that are not true, that are not life, and that are not from God. Which then led me to question whether the things I know to be true in my life were God's truth or my truth. Have I given everything to God?

Sometimes, it's not about what God is going to show up and do. He's not going to come in and make the decision for us. He's not going to plan everything out for us. He will leave us in a situation and allow us to make a decision. It is when we make that decision that he will step in; although he already knows, he wants to see our level of commitment. Sometimes, I look back and think, *Woah. You have been to hell and back Sam, why are you here smiling girl? What is your problem? Go roll around on the floor crying, in self-pity, for a few days* - and I did. I honestly did. For forty-eight hours. Then, I woke up reminded that I am a daughter of someone who is bigger than this whole situation. I am not defined by this. I am not destined for this. And I am certainly not going to live in this. This is not going to destroy me. And literally, in that moment, everything changed. - Faith awakened. Joy rose up inside me. Peace flowed abundantly over me. And I was filled - filled with the spirit of a God who is able to do immeasurably more than I can think or imagine. No, it's not like that every single day of the week, and for me to say or suggest that would be wrong. But yes, I have access to that at all times. I have full access, VIP entry to the gifts of God. Sometimes, it's good to hurt. It reminds us that there is something wrong. There is something, or someone, to pray for. There is something that needs to CHANGE. Change often brings up questions, and questions lead to more questions, but then, hopefully, answers. Right now, I am seeing lots of answers to prayer! God is speaking to me about why things happen and how he wants things to go, moving forward. He is a great restorer and I totally believe that he will speak life into dry bones. It is in those times that our foundations are strengthened and we are empowered to speak what we know to be truth over our lives. For us to profess hope into a desperate situation. For us to be reminded that a) it is ok to not be ok, and b) to know that there has to be a change. That something has to shift. That a new choice has to be made. And the choice that I choose to make is that I will always choose joy.

Who knows what is going to happen going forward. I know that God doesn't want me to give up. That he has directed my steps in a particular way, and that I was created for something pretty epic and amazing (as tough as it is). I know that in the past year I have been in countless situations where I have only been able to depend on God. I found myself homeless twice, and on one occasion, I literally sat in my office until 10 p.m. not knowing where I would spend the night. And that's ok – Mary and Joseph didn't know where they would spend their night, but God showed up and directed their steps in his timing, in his provision, in his grace. I wouldn't change that, or sacrifice that. I have walked away from people that I valued and respected more than I actually imagined, because God opened my eyes to things unseen. He used them to help me appreciate what I had, especially in my Husband. He gave me a supernatural ability to have different perspectives and understanding in regard to why people do the things they do, and why it is they find themselves in some situations where they face the right thing and not the easy thing. It has, by far, been the toughest year of my life, but I am thankful. I am thankful, because I have been able to share it with you. To journey it with people, and to know that God never leaves me on my own.

So as you move on to the last chapter of this book, to the altar call, I leave you on the day of my one year anniversary to remind you … anything is possible with God. Don't limit your dreams, and don't run because of trials. Keep fighting. Keep pressing forward! And keep believing that God will show up, because he will! In ways you couldn't even imagine. My Marriage is restored!

Grace > Conflict

CHAPTER 21

Look beside you

Recently, a thought that has plagued my mind is the statement, 'I feel so far from God'. This is an evidently valid feeling. It is stated that Jesus fills the gap, so there has to be a gap of which we feel. But knowing God, and knowing his attributes, made me question the statement, and how I perceived it. Is it that we feel far from God, or is it that we have allowed sin to make us stupid? Stupid enough to ignore God trying to communicate with us. I know God is always there. He goes before me. He stands next to me. And he is pulling up the ranks behind me. So how can I feel far away from him? Knowing that there are points throughout my walk where I have suffered the feeling of great distance from my mighty creator, I thought back to these times and questioned what it was that made me feel so far away from God. My answer was this: Lack of fellowship. The times in my life where I felt like our mighty God and myself were worlds apart, have been the times where I have tried to fight alone. Not only without God, but without the support from Jesus' bride. From people who were placed around me to love and care for me like God loves and cares for me. To show me his astounding love that we cannot be separated from, not by life or death or our fears for today or worries from tomorrow. If nothing can separate us from his love then when we feel so distant from him, it has to be something we ourselves are doing, and we ourselves can change. Removing myself from fellowship has been a very apparent way of widening the gap between me and my saviour. A very wide door which is swinging open for a multitude of things to enter, feeling far from God being one of them. The second thing that was very apparent to me when I thought of times of loneliness (because in reality we never are really alone), I thought what other fruit had I cut from the tree to distance myself from the root. Giving time to listen to God? Checked that box. When I feel lonely, it's because I'm doing all the talking and not doing any listening. This would drive a great divide between any relationship on earth, and with our heavenly father. So why do we not listen for God? God is probably, at these times, screaming out his love for us, and we are choosing to ignore him and his perfect will for us. Nevertheless, we will pour out our troubles and worries at the foot of the cross, and expect all the answers to appear like rain in a drought. How foolish are we?

Some of you reading this may not understand the transformation I have experienced. You may also think that the life I used to lead was perfectly fine, and that some of the things I got up to are your idea of fun and games. I see where you're coming from. I've been there, living for the next best thing, the next buzz I could get, the next boy, the next drink, the next drug, but take this as *my desperate plea*! Turn away. Turn away from the pain and hurt you feel when rejected by society for trying too hard to fit in. From the mornings of regret waking up in random people's beds, feeling like death warmed up. My plea that there is a love out there that no man, drink, drug, person, or situation will *ever* substitute, will never be as fulfilling as the love from your Father who sits in heaven waiting for you. The one whom he sent to fill the gap that you yourself fill with so much earthly waste. Take this as my plea of realisation that living your life for the Lord brings meaning, brings purpose, and brings a sense of something better. You will literally see heaven on earth. You will learn to appreciate what little you have, and love those who already surround you. You will see life in a whole different way, with a rose tint. No, I'm not saying it's going to be easy. God loves us too much to keep us the way we are. Knowing God means growing. Growing into what he created us to be, what he longs for us to be. Please, just remember that we spend more time beyond the grave than we do before it. Where do you want to spend your eternity? Nothing on this earth will ensure heaven as part of the parcel of leading a good life. But knowing Jesus and the sacrifice he made for YOU, each of you individually, with all your faults and failures, with all your wrongs and pains. Knowing the deepest darkest places of your soul, he still chose to die for YOU! Please don't let traditionalism push you away for what God has in store. Don't let people with their 'earthly given right to Judge you' do this also, because the one person whose judgement you should care about doesn't judge. Instead, he loves you. All of you.

So please, take these words, this book, my story as my desperate plea to you. here is nowhere so dark that the lord *cannot* rescue you by grace. Because grace is *greater than* …

You were made for such a time as this …

About the Author

Thankful that God doesn't call people that are qualified but he qualifies the called. He blessed me with the ability to get things down on paper better than I can communicate them in any other way. Originally from the Lake District UK and married to Demichael who is from Cincinnati OH.

Lightning Source UK Ltd.
Milton Keynes UK
UKOW04f1222070316

269742UK00001BA/254/P